ALSO BY KAY ALLENBAUGH

Chocolate for a Woman's Soul

Chocolate for a Woman's Heart

Chocolate for a Lover's Heart

Chocolate for a Mother's Heart

Chocolate for a Woman's Spirit

Chocolate for a Teen's Soul

Chocolate for a Woman's Blessings

Chocolate for a Teen's Heart

Chocolate for a Woman's Dreams

Chocolate for a Teen's Spirit

Chocolate for a Woman's Courage

HEARTWARMING STORIES

ABOUT MAKING YOUR WISHES

COME TRUE

A FIRESIDE BOOK
Published by Simon & Schuster
New York   London   Toronto   Sydney   Singapore

CHOCOLATE
for a
TEEN'S
DREAMS

KAY ALLENBAUGH

FIRESIDE
Rockefeller Center
1230 Avenue of the Americas
New York, NY 10020

For information regarding special discounts for bulk purchases, please contact
Simon & Schuster Special Sales at 1-800-456-6798 or
business@simonandschuster.com

Manufactured in the United States of America

1   3   5   7   9   10   8   6   4   2

Library of Congress Cataloging-in-Publication Data
Chocolate for a teen's dreams : heartwarming stories about making
your wishes come true / [compiled by] Kay Allenbaugh.
p.   cm.
Summary: A collection of real-life stories written by teenage girls and women
relating their dreams concerning such things as love, friendship, and recognition
of their talents, and how they make dreams and wishes come true.
1. Teenage girls—Psychology.   2. Teenage girls—Conduct of life.
3. Interpersonal relations in adolescence.   [1. Teenage girls—Conduct of life.
2. Self-actualization (Psychology).   3. Interpersonal relations.]
I. Allenbaugh, Kay.
HQ798 .C546   2003
305.235—dc21   2002191183
ISBN 0-7432-3703-X

This book is dedicated with love

to the young at heart in my life

who have made my dreams come true—

Nicholas Shea Allenbaugh and Elva Sue Bain

CONTENTS

III
FITS AND STARTS

IV
MORE THAN ENOUGH

V
YOUNG WISDOM ROCKS

VI
WHY ME?

VII

ANGELS HERE AND THERE

CHOCOLATE
for a
TEEN'S
DREAMS

INTRODUCTION

re you dreaming enough?
Some of us dream awake. Some of us dream asleep. Our dreams—those wishes we hold most dear to our hearts—create the passion for us to have a rich life. We all love to dream!

Chocolate for a Teen's Dreams celebrates our power to envision what we want with heartwarming stories by teens and women remembering their teens. They have had many different kinds of dreams—both little and big. Whether they are seeking a rite of passage, true love, a best friend, a date to the prom, or recognition of their talents, they share their most poignant and memorable moments with you. You will see that dreams don't just have to be hazy wishes; they can come true!

In real life, dreams motivate us to move ahead. Even with our best intentions, maintaining optimism can be difficult in our fast-paced and sometimes painful world, and it can be hard to make progress toward our goals except in fits and starts. Yet, with a clear vision in mind, we want to move ahead. The "Chocolate" contributors share all they can about turning a dream into a vision and a vision into a reality. They show that a steadfast belief in yourself is a practice made perfect.

In addition to faith in ourselves, though, we also need the support of family and friends, as well as stories like these to remind us of all the amazing possibilities that await us. Find the richness in joining a group of friends or a mentor who truly has your best interests at heart. Share your wisdom. Help one another. And be sure to celebrate your accomplishments, finding the good in all that happens. Believe for each other when one of you is down. Comfort and remind each other of your strengths—you are always more than enough! And when you need a good laugh, do something silly together. Create a ritual for the special times when one of you has an important event or needs additional support. You may want to light a candle for yourself or your friend, setting the intention that all will go as you wish.

With that sense of triumph in your heart, find a cozy place to be with a friend or to relax in peaceful solitude. Nibble a piece of chocolate and savor these pages that are written just for you. Dream along with the "Chocolate sisterhood" who created this sacred space. May you learn through these stories how to nurture and grow your wishes in order to make them come true. Sweet dreams!

I
IN THE NAME
OF LOVE

When wonder and love become as indispensable to you
as foundation and blush,
you will become the most radiant woman in the world.

SARAH BAN BREATHNACH

WORTH FIGHTING FOR

Although he wasn't every girl's dream guy, Rich was everything to me. He wasn't tall, just about my height. And he wasn't built well; he was very thin. In fact, he wasn't even that good-looking, but he had a smile that melted my heart. His green-brown eyes would sparkle, lighting his whole face as a collection of dimples revealed themselves. I found his smile irresistible.

We met at a practice for our school musical. He was a junior playing a lead role. I was a freshman, delegated to the chorus. The first time I saw him, I fell instantly in love.

Another girl at play practice, Dani, had a crush on Rich, too. Although she was a freshman like me, she was not nearly as innocent and naïve as me. She had been around the block several times with several others, and she wanted to take Rich for a test-drive. And no wide-eyed goody-goody was going to stand in her way.

During our last practice before spring break, Dani told a friend of mine that she would fight me for Rich. When I heard this, I nearly died. *Do people really do that?* I wondered. *I thought it was just in movies—bad ones.* I hid in the shadows all night, making every effort to avoid Dani.

Finally, practice was over and spring break began. When I told my brother, Joe, what happened, he agreed to teach me to fight so that I could stand up for myself if Dani came around.

"You'll still get creamed," he said, "but at least you won't look like too much of an idiot."

Joe invited his friend Dave over, and together they taught me

everything, from making a fist to firing a final blow (in the un-
likely event that I would win). We had daily sparring matches that
left me bruised both in body and spirit. I still could not believe that
someone wanted to fight with me—and that I was thinking of
going through with it.

When school started again, I was consumed with what might
happen at practice. I did nothing but rehearse in my mind what I
learned over the break.

Finally, classes ended and I headed to the auditorium. Dani was
nowhere in sight. *What a relief! Maybe she's sick,* I thought. Then I
realized that Rich wasn't there, either. I had seen him in school, so
I knew he wasn't sick. It wasn't like him to skip practice. Where
was he?

One of Rich's friends came up to me and said, "If you're looking for Rich, he went for a walk with Dani."

My heart sank. He couldn't. He wouldn't. How dare he! Was he
just playing me? Did they plan this together so they could laugh
at me?

I ran to the balcony. I wasn't sure if the tears that fell were from
hurt, anger, or embarrassment. Then, through wet lashes, I saw
them walk into the auditorium, exchange a few whispers, and
hug. She immediately went over to her friends and I vaguely
heard the word "kiss." I felt as though I had been run over by a
truck.

Tears flowed in endless streams, running down my nose and
cheeks, salting my lips. I didn't even hear the balcony door open. I
jumped when I felt someone touch my shoulder.

It was Rich. "What's the matter, Lis?" he asked innocently.

I wanted so badly to be brave, to make up a story and pretend I
was a character in a play. My grandfather died? My parents are getting a divorce? I had to think of something quick.

"I really thought you liked me. But you went for a walk with
Dani. She wanted to fight me. I practiced all during break so I
could fight for you."

Rich laughed silently as I spoke. I was so embarrassed, but I kept talking.

"Was it all a joke?" I asked him. "How could you do this to me? Why didn't you just tell me you wanted to be with her?"

He wiped my tears with one hand and held me close with the other. "Lis, I took the walk with Dani to tell her I wanted to be with you. I told her that I like who I am when I'm with you. I told her I wanted to take you to the prom."

"Then why would you hug and kiss her?" I demanded, not even hearing his last sentence.

"She said she wanted closure or something, so I gave her a peck on the cheek and a goodbye hug. That's all. It's you I want to be with. Will you go to the prom with me?"

This time I heard him. The tears of pain turned to tears of joy. "I would love to," I said, and we hugged.

I floated through the next few weeks. The play was a huge success, but that didn't matter to me. What mattered was that I would be going to the prom with Rich.

Then, on that warm April night, I went on my first date with my first love. And, as we danced closely in the dim light, Rich leaned in and gave me my first kiss—and it wasn't a little peck on the cheek like he had given Dani.

As the kiss ended, he looked at me and flashed one of his amazing smiles. It was then that I knew that he was worth fighting for.

LISA SANDERS

Horses make a landscape more beautiful.
ALICE WALKER

OF HORSES AND DREAMS

Like many girls growing up, I was certifiably horse crazy. I'm not sure when it began, but my parents soon gave up all hope that it was a passing fancy.

One Christmas a couple of years later, they rewarded my persistence with a crotchety little Shetland pony named Sally. Sally was not fond of children and she had no intention of participating in my Black Beauty fantasies. Many of my early riding experiences involved being brushed off under low-hanging trees as my "trusty steed" bolted back to the barn.

Thankfully, it didn't take me long to outgrow Sally and graduate to my first "real" horse, a beautiful Arabian named Sunfire. A bay, his brown color shone like a copper penny in the sunlight. My parents resigned themselves to what would be several years of lessons, vet bills, shows, and everything in between.

At the same time, I was trying to find my place at school. Some say high school years are the "best years of your life," but those words must only be true for homecoming queens or the captain of the football team. They weren't true for me, a skinny wallflower who wasn't exceptional in anything school related. Forget about fitting in, I wanted to just plain hide, which can be difficult when you are nearly six feet tall by the eighth grade! The girls around me seemed prettier, smarter, and more desirable; to make matters worse, I often paired myself with the most petite friends who made me feel twice as big and graceless. How I longed for a place where I could shine, where my unknown talents would be discovered like buried treasure and revealed for all to see. I experimented with playing a musical instrument and going out for various sports (basketball should have been natural for someone my height!), but nothing felt right. Nothing, that is, except horseback riding.

Eventually, 4-H activities gave me a way to excel. I qualified for a place on the state fair team two years in a row, and I took lessons in dressage and jumping, and I competed in local shows and parades. On my horse I felt confident and natural. I didn't have to be a cheerleader or captain of the debate team to ride well.

When my first boyfriend dumped me at fourteen for my best friend, I found solace with my horse, whose muzzle, soft and smooth as a baby's cheek, nosed away my tears. And after an argument with family or friends, I could always find a new perspective on life after spending a little time in the barn with Sunfire. Caring for Sunny filled me with pride for doing something I was good at instead of constantly comparing myself with those around me.

Sunny used to come when I called. We had a field that was very wooded, and I'd walk in the gate and just call his name a few times. You could hear his galloping hooves before you actually saw him.

On weekends, Sunny and I would take long rides—just the two of us—and I'd reward him by stopping at a special spot where he could munch on crab apples that fell from the tree. One Christmas Eve, my sister and I went out around midnight to ride bareback. Snow had just fallen and the moon was shining so brightly that it looked like day. The air was very still and crisp and the horses pranced along, snorting their frosty breath in the air. Sitting on Sunny, then, was like riding a bear with his woolly winter coat keeping my legs warm.

In my junior year my family relocated and the horses were sold. When the trailer came for my beautiful Arabian, Sunfire, I thought my heart would break. More than just an animal or hobby, he was my faithful companion and I knew my life would never be the same.

Those years are long past now, but the wonderful memories remain. I can't imagine any place on earth more comforting than a barn full of horses. The sounds of swishing tails in cozy stalls and sniffling noses searching for lost bits of grain. The good smell of fresh hay, sweet molasses oats mixed with oiled leather. And the barn cats, regal as kings, surveying their world atop thrones of hay.

I look forward to the future when my life will once again be touched by a horse. It is something I hope to share with my own daughter who, like me, may one day sit astride a beautiful horse and feel like she belongs there.

CATHERINE MADERA

LABELS AND LOVE

I *was fifteen years old that summer and on my first* trip away from home without my parents. One of the school clubs I belonged to held a national convention. I, along with more than one thousand other high school students from across the nation, spent a week living in a college dorm, using the facilities of Indiana University for academic competitions, athletic events, seminars, workshops, and evening dances.

To my peers at home I was a "brain." They had decided early on that I was a "goody-goody," useful only for answers to homework assignments and labor on group projects. I'm confident that I was well liked, but I was not socially popular. Weekend parties, dance invitations, even the coveted back seats of the bus on field trips, were never made available to me. Too, I was caught up in the love songs on the radio and the romances that played out on the movie screens. Like most girls my age, I dreamed of falling in love. The boys I knew, however, were after the popular girls, the cheerleaders, the athletes, and the social butterflies. Definitely not me. I wasn't unhappy, but I did wish I fit in better. My days were filled, though, with school and homework, a part-time job, weekend trips to the mall, sleepovers with my best girlfriend, and myriad extracurricular activities.

The first few days of the convention rushed by as I went from one activity to the next. I was meeting people from different states, learning new things, and enjoying not only the vastness and beauty of the college campus, but also a newfound feeling of anonymity. No one here, save for the few classmates I traveled with, knew me. The words "goody-goody" and "brain" were not stamped on my forehead. My identification badge identified me simply as a delegate from Illinois.

As I met people, I realized that I would not forever be bound to the labels bestowed on me by my peers. What a rush it was to walk into the cafeteria and have a new friend wave me down, making space at the table so that I could join the conversation. I was invited to late-night card games and even asked if I would be at the dances. Me! The week was passing much too quickly.

Then it happened.

One afternoon, midway through the convention, a classmate and I were heading over to the student center to go bowling. As we left the dorm, we realized that our identification badges were back in our room. Since we needed them in order to bowl, we turned and headed back up the sidewalk, running smack into a couple of boys who we knew, from their badges, were also part of the convention. We excused ourselves and continued up the sidewalk, but as we stepped inside, I turned to get a second look at one of the boys only to see him turn around to take a look at me!

I never did get to the bowling alley that day, sending my classmate ahead while I took the time to make some new acquaintances. By the end of the afternoon, I had a whole circle of friends from Florida, including David. He and I were soon teasing each other and laughing like old friends. We went to that night's scheduled entertainment—a talent show—together, and I thought I would melt when, in the darkness of the theater, he slipped his arm around my shoulder. Hand in hand, we walked across campus together, and I was stunned when he kissed me goodnight at the steps of my dorm. I'm not sure I slept that night, as I relived the events of the day over and over again.

There were only two days of the convention left, and while we continued to enjoy all the activities, David and I were inseparable. The final night's dance was a semi-formal, and for the first (and what would turn out to be the only) time in my high school career, I had a date. Not a blind date, not a date with a friend, but an honest to goodness date with a boy who wanted to be with me that night.

The morning we said goodbye to each other, David and I made no promises or commitments. Living in Florida and Illinois wouldn't exactly give us the chance to continue our budding romance. I cried, he looked miserable, and we defied convention rules by stealing a marathon goodbye kiss in his dorm room.

I returned home with a broken heart and a new outlook. I had learned that there was so much more to life than the limited social structure contained by the walls of my high school. I had gained confidence in myself, and I knew that I needed neither to fit in nor to accept the judgment of my peers at home. I had been shown that I had other peers (boys, even!) who sought my company simply because I was me. While I enjoyed the rest of my time in high school, I looked forward to moving on.

David and I did keep in touch, "lighting the postal system on fire," as my best friend used to tease. At first our letters were the stuff of soap opera romance, dripping with sentimentality, full of "I miss you," "I love you," and "I can't wait to see you again." A few months after we said goodbye, though, the frequency of our letters decreased, and we went on with our lives, never again anything more than friends.

Maybe it was because I felt an emotional pull to the place. Of course, the quality of its academic program was undeniable. Whatever my reasons, three years later I would once again find myself on the campus of Indiana University, this time as a college freshman. Once my parents had helped me unpack my stuff and had gone home, I set out alone and rode my bicycle through the campus, taking a tour of my past and finding, once again, the rush of exhilaration that came with the feeling of anonymity.

I returned to my dorm that night ready to mold my life to my own image, ready to meet people who knew nothing about me, and ready to succeed. And, if ever I were to doubt myself, I needed only the memories of that one magical week of friendships and stolen kisses to remind me that not only was I capable of finding happiness, I was worthy of it.

JENNIFER DOLOSKI

Heed the still, small voice
that so seldom leads us wrong, and never into folly.
MME. DUDEVANT

CROSSROADS

W*e sat in the parking lot of a neighborhood pub*
as we had done twice before. We had planned to
grab a sandwich, talk a while, and relax after a
tiring week of work and school. Only I wasn't relaxed. I was ready
to cry.

"I have to tell you something," I said to Nick. I held his arm, preventing him from opening the car door.

Nick looked confused and serious, an expression far different
from the usual cheerful smile he wore. I looked into his handsome
face, trying to find the words to tell him that we couldn't go out
together anymore. My boyfriend, Armando, wanted me to stop
seeing my friend Nick, and tonight I had to tell him. What else
could I do?

I had known Nick Bertrand since I was a junior high school brat
and had hung around my big brother and his friends. Nick had always been nice to the "kid sister," teaching me to play cards,
cheering me up when I had my tonsils out, and taking me to play
tennis during the summer after my first teen heartbreak.

When I met Armando during senior year and we dated as
steadies, Nick still attended my high school graduation and came

to the family party afterward. I told Armando (and myself) that Nick was like another big brother to me. I didn't want to admit that I had always carried a "crush" for him. When he told me at my graduation party that he would be leaving in a week to attend a university in another town, I felt a sadness I couldn't explain.

Over the years, my relationship with Armando grew more serious as we attended college together. He came to work for my father and we saw marriage in our future. Then during my last college semester, Nick came home to accept a teaching position and football coaching assignment at a local high school. We met up again one Sunday in September outside the church. I was so excited to see him and couldn't wait to show him the pretty opal ring Armando had given me, and to tell him why I had decided to become a teacher.

Nick and I stood outside church for two hours and tried to catch up on the past four years. We met every Sunday morning for two months, progressing from talking outside, to sitting together during Mass, and going out together for breakfast afterward.

Armando preferred to work on Sunday mornings and to spend the afternoons watching football games. Even though Nick loved sports, he didn't want to watch them on TV anymore. Coaching football six days a week motivated Nick to find other things to do on his free Sundays. So we went miniature golfing together and to movie matinees. We talked over sundaes, took walks around the lake, and chatted on my parents' front porch.

One afternoon when I was sick in bed with a bad cold, my mother brought me a sandwich and took the time to sit on my bed. "Nick is a good family friend. I don't want you to hurt him. You need to be considerate of his feelings for you."

I was surprised by her implication. "Nick and I are just friends, Mom."

"But what about Armando?" she asked. "You've been dating for years. I thought you two were getting married. He won't like all the time you spend with Nick."

"Don't worry, Mom. Everything is just fine," I told her, but her cautionary words started me thinking seriously about my relationships with both men.

After a college buddy saw Nick and me at the movies, Armando seemed very jealous of my friendship with Nick. "I don't want you to go out with him anymore. It looks bad. You belong to me." However, he didn't offer to change the way our relationship had fallen into a predictable pattern. He liked that he worked for my father and that we were the only "steady" couple among our college friends.

Armando was nice looking, had a good work ethic, and was comfortable at family gatherings. He drove a dependable car, laughed at my jokes, and didn't mind if I found other things to do on Sundays during football season. Why would I want to change the relationship that had been a continuous part of my life for four years? Everything had progressed as it was supposed to in a serious relationship between two people. I was wearing a beautiful "promise" ring from Armando, wasn't I?

But that night, outside the pub, I didn't have the ring on my hand. I never wore it when I was with Nick. There was nothing tangible to remind me of Armando. Our relationship had become more routine than romantic, and I opened myself up to the possibility of change.

As I held Nick's arm to stop him from leaving the car, I realized what I had been denying for years. I couldn't end my friendship with Nick because I needed to see him every day of my life. I loved Nick's sense of humor, the way he listened earnestly to everything I said, and the way he made me feel like a person who mattered.

He was my best friend in the world, and thoughts of losing him melted into the hot tears rolling down my face. "Oh, Nick, I just can't stop seeing you!"

Naturally he embraced me, and I told him about Armando's demands, sobbing against his shirt. I told him how I felt confused and sad. Who knows how long I talked, and if any 'of it made sense. But Nick listened, like always, until I finally reached my personal crossroads of emotions, words, and actions. I had to make my choice.

I sat up to stare into those expressive green eyes that led the way into his heart. "The truth is, Nick, that I love you more than Armando, and if there's someone who needs to step out of my life, it's him, not you."

Nick's smile appeared, and he said, "Do you know that every Sunday in church, I prayed for your happiness? And I'd tell God, 'but if she isn't happy with Armando, then I want her. I want her.'"

That's when we first kissed like two people who had discovered they were deeply in love with each other. And we've been together ever since.

That night I took responsibility for my own personal happiness. I also learned how to listen to myself and to speak from my heart. And most important, I realized that when God is the matchmaker, love is never "routine."

DIANE GONZALES BERTRAND

MY MOTHER'S CAT

When my nineteen-year-old mother died two weeks after giving birth to me, I inherited her cat, Paprika. He was a gentle giant, with deep orange stripes and large, yellow eyes that gazed at me tolerantly, as I dragged him around wherever I went.

Paprika was ten years old when I came into this world. He had been held and loved by my mother for ten years of his life, while I had never known her. I considered him my link to her. Each time I hugged him tightly to my chest, I was warmed by the knowledge that she had done so, too.

"Did you love her a lot?" I would often ask Paprika, as we snuggled on my bed.

"Meow!" he would answer, rubbing my chin with his pink nose.

"Do you miss her?"

"Meow!"

"I miss her, too, even though I didn't know her. But Grandma says she is in heaven and is watching over us from there. I think it makes her happy that we have each other," I would always say, for it was a most comforting thought to my childish mind.

"Meow!" Paprika would respond, climbing on my chest and purring contentedly. I was convinced he understood me, and I knew I understood him.

At that time we lived in the country of my birth, Hungary, and my maternal grandparents were raising me because World War II had taken my young father away. As I grew, the war intensified, and soon we were forced to become migrants in search of safer surroundings.

In the spring of 1944 when I was seven, as we traveled in a wooden wagon pulled by two horses, Paprika and I snuggled in the back of the wagon. During the numerous air raids of those times, when we had to scramble to find safety in a cellar, closet, or ditch, he was always in my arms, for I refused to go without him. How could I, when one of the first stories I was ever told as a child was that of my dying mother begging her parents to take care of her baby as well as her cat?

During the Soviet occupation of our country in the early spring of 1945, as we emerged from a bunker where we had spent a terror-filled night, Paprika made friends with a young Russian soldier. He treated Paprika to tins of sardines because he reminded him of his own cat back in Russia. Through the trying times that persisted in our country, Paprika's love made things easier for me to bear.

By the fall of 1945, Grandfather had gone into hiding to avoid being imprisoned as a dissident by the new communist government. The solemn Christmas Grandmother and I expected turned into my worst nightmare when I awoke on Christmas morning to find Paprika, still curled up next to me, lifeless and cold. He was nineteen years old. I was nine, and I vowed never to give my heart to another cat.

Christmas 1951 was our first Christmas in our wonderful new country, the United States of America. The horrors of war, the four years of hardship in a refugee camp were behind us now, and a new life filled with hope lay ahead.

On that Christmas morning, I awoke to a tantalizing aroma wafting through the house. Grandmother was cooking her first American turkey. And one of the presents under the Christmas tree seemed alive, for it was hopping around to the tune of "Jingle Bells" playing on the radio. I rushed over, pulled off the orange bow, and took the lid off the box.

"Meow," cried the present, jumping straight into my lap and purring. It was a tiny, orange tabby kitten. When I looked into its yellow eyes, the old vow I had made in 1945 crumbled away and love filled my heart once again. I do believe that my mother smiled down at us from heaven, approvingly, that Christmas Day.

RENIE SZILAK BURGHARDT

TIPS FOR TEEN DREAMS

1. Focus on your dream. Plot a course that will help you reach it and then begin to take small steps down the path.
2. Identify and develop your talents. It takes a lot of courage, but if you do, opportunities will come your way!
3. If you are feeling troubled or uncertain, find a quiet place that nurtures your peace of mind.
4. Read inspirational stories. They remind you of what is possible in your life.
5. Act wisely! When your actions match your values you are paving the way toward your goal.
6. When a dream comes true, celebrate!
7. Laugh yourself silly at least once every day.
8. Expect miracles! God has a plan for each of us, and that includes you!
9. When you have doubts, ask someone you trust to believe for you.
10. Discover what brings you joy because happiness comes from the inside.
11. Eat a little chocolate! It will release endorphins and lift your spirits.
12. Do not judge others. If you are judgmental, it says more about you than about anyone you have judged.
13. Good choices lead to bigger dreams.
14. Replace each negative thought you have about yourself with two that are positive. If you can change your thinking, you can change your life!

15. Take care of yourself as if you were your best friend (because you are).
16. Thank your parents for *something* on a regular basis.
17. If you get stuck, seek the advice of a wise woman.
18. Look back at the first goal you accomplished and realize how far you have come!
19. Remember to say your prayers.

KAY ALLENBAUGH

THE PIANO LESSON

My piano teacher, Karen Joseph, had little time to notice the adoration of a hormonal teenage girl who rarely practiced her music lessons. Karen stuffed her days to overflowing as a young wife, new mother, piano teacher, church organist, and performer on the local Christian TV station.

In our little Ohio farming community, everyone knew Karen. The older folks watched her grow up, playing the piano 'by ear' at the age of two and serving as the town's only prodigy. "Perfect pitch," her peers whispered. The kids gawked. They knew she had talent.

When I knocked on Karen's door every Wednesday afternoon, I clutched a yellow piano book in one hand and my $1.50 payment in the other. Like a postman I came—rain, shine, winter, summer. But my adolescent interests involved love and marriage, intimacy and relationships, not piano.

Karen had recently moved back home from the state capital so I didn't know all her life's details. It didn't matter because I dreamily sketched them in. I looked at the picture hanging on the wall beside the piano. She posed in her tulle-skirted, spaghetti-strapped wedding dress. I imagined her romantic fairy tale wedding. My virginal thoughts skittered over the specifics of the honeymoon, content to wrap it in an aura of love and romance in a tropical setting.

Alan, her handsome, broad-shouldered husband, came home most days for lunch. In the summer, I edged past him in the doorway as his noon hour ended and my lesson began. With imagination roaring in overdrive, I looked over my shoulder at him, wondering. Sometimes, I searched Karen's face for love signs. But catching a glimpse of swollen lips or dreamy doe eyes was difficult as she rushed me to the studio piano in the living room.

She told me to play my lesson while she returned to the kitchen to clean. A quick glance through the adjoining door revealed a chubby baby who wore more of her food on the outside than inside.

While I played, Karen put her daughter down for a nap. All the time she called out comments and observations. "You missed a sharp there . . . Wait, do that passage again and don't rush it . . . Keep your triplets even . . . Have you been practicing your fingering?"

She knew. Even from the kitchen with a squirming baby in her arms, she knew when I hadn't practiced.

By the time I finished the first song, the baby was usually slurping on a bottle in her crib. Karen perched on the edge of a folding chair beside the piano with a cup of coffee balanced on her knee. Perfume, Tabu, swirled around her, freshly applied atop the scent of talcum powder and baby food. She swiped at wispy curls then settled back to listen.

Music was her language and she spoke it fluently, greeting each song as if it were an old friend. I confronted them with an adversarial karate chop. But Karen patiently pointed me toward perfection, unaware that I had questions to ask that involved men and women not notes and time signatures.

I lived with an older brother and parents who seemed ancient. I could never imagine my mom and dad 'doing it' and didn't want to. But Karen, a young woman with a baby, was obviously experienced.

She knew the secrets of a world I longed to experience. When did she turn into a woman? That's what I wanted to know. How did she know she was in love? How did she attract her husband?

What was it like to live with a man? What was it like to wake up with a man? With that last thought, I blushed and stumbled over a key change.

"Sorry," I murmured.

"That's okay, you'll learn," she said.

When, I wanted to ask. *When will I be just like you?*

One Wednesday at the end of my lesson, Karen asked, "Could you stay with Jennifer for a few hours?" The TV station had called, wanting Karen to fill in at a taping session at the last minute. She needed a baby-sitter.

I, with no baby-sitting experience, hesitated. But how hard could it be to hang out with a sleeping baby? Besides, Mom was a couple blocks away.

"Yeah, sure. I'll baby-sit."

The mysterious life of a young family unfolded before me as Karen drove away. I touched the back of the chair where the handsome husband probably sat. I blushed as I peeked into their bedroom. But before my imagination could swamp me in a tide of raging hormones, the baby wailed.

Panicked, I ran to her crib, cringing as the odor of messy diaper hit me. Not just a messy diaper, a messy bed and messy baby as well. Little Jennifer put her heart and lungs into her misery, pausing only to vomit over my shoulder.

My romantic notions of motherhood and wifedom popped like water balloons. I awkwardly wrapped a couple of blankets around the angry, drippy baby and phoned home. Mom arrived, laughing, a few minutes later and cleaned up the mess before Karen returned.

While listening for the sound of Karen's footsteps on the porch, I looked around her little love nest. My thoughts scurried ahead of me on my way home fifteen minutes later. I clutched my earnings, plus a generous tip, and pondered what I'd earned and what I'd learned. Something happens after that fairy tale happily-ever-after ending that I hadn't considered.

At home, I headed for the piano before the door banged shut behind me. I'd start with the C scales, I decided, and work my way up to Bach.

DAWN GOLDSMITH

II
A RITE OF PASSAGE

Don't wait. Set out . . . it might just be a magic day.

Nancy Coey

COCONUT SURPRISE

I've heard that for some people, becoming an adult is something that happens gradually, imperceptibly, over time. Others, like me, have one defining moment when adulthood smacks us upside the head and says, "This is it!"

It happened to me while I was away at college. Being a sophomore, I'd already had more than a year's worth of practice at doing my own laundry, paying my own phone bills, and dragging myself out of bed to get to my 8:30 A.M. classes on time. All in all, I felt pretty grown up and responsible, as if I knew what it meant to be an adult. That was before the moth fiasco.

My roommate and I had noticed our dorm room being shared by a sprinkling of tiny, pale moths, each no more than a centimeter long. It seemed there were always one or two little moths fluttering around the room, and while in the beginning I thought their presence was sort of quaint, it soon became annoying. I found myself smashing a lot of little moths with my textbooks. Heartless, perhaps, but it's hard to study with bugs whizzing by your nose.

One day, after my roommate had gone to class and I was trying to study at my desk, I noticed a moth that had been rude enough to invite at least four of his friends to my room without asking. Exasperated, I got up to see if I could find a crack in the wall or some other place where the moths might be finding their way into the room. I wandered around, checking in back of furniture, studying the window ledges, and finally, opening my desk drawers.

When I yanked open the bottom drawer, I discovered the kind of horror that gives Stephen King nightmares. There, nestled inside what had once been a fresh-from-the-tree, whole coconut—yes, I said coconut—was a colony of squirming moth larvae. Dozens of slimy-looking, worm-like creatures oozed out of cracks in the coconut from all directions. They writhed beside moths in various stages of metamorphosis, from semi-shelled pupae that looked like greasy pill capsules to sticky-winged juvenile moths coated in films of mucus. As the larvae wiggled through the layers of slime, and the larger moths crawled past them, I stood horrified. It was like watching a scene out of the movie *Aliens*.

Vaguely, I remembered my mother sending me the coconut and some plastic leis with the suggestion that I host a beach party in my dorm room. Thinking that the idea was cute but too lazy to follow through, I had tossed the coconut in my drawer and forgotten about it. Big mistake.

A mucus-coated moth gained its strength, fluttering out of the drawer toward my face. Have you ever had a nightmare where you couldn't scream? This was like that. I was so freaked out I could hardly move, let alone scream. I staggered backward and tried not to hyperventilate.

I had to get this *thing* out of my room, and fast, but there was no one there to help me. No parents, no authority figures, not even my roommate. My first urge was to leave the dorm until I could locate the nearest adult, drag the person into my room, point at the mass of wriggling slime, and scream, but the scary truth was that I was going to have to handle this by myself.

I stood there panting, eyes glazed. There was an extra-large garbage can in the community area of my dorm floor, but getting the "hive" from my room to the garbage can was going to require picking the thing up and taking it all the way down the hall and through the lobby.

I can do this, I thought. *I have to do this.* A mantra formed in my mind, and I said it out loud. "I'm mature, I'm an adult, I can handle this." I had to actually hear the words to make them real. "I'm mature, I'm an adult, I can handle this," I repeated as I walked to my door and propped it open in preparation for the sprint I was about to make. "I'm mature, I'm an adult, I can handle this," I repeated as I crouched close to the colony of writhing worms. I put my hands near either side of the coconut and managed to pick it up with only my ten fingernails touching its decaying shell. My breathing was quick and panicky. I whimpered as I peeled the coconut away from the pool of sticky bug-and-fruit goo coating my desk drawer.

I stood up and held the thing at arm's length, trying to avoid the larvae crawling near my fingers and the tiny moths flitting around my face.

"I'm mature, I'm an adult, I can handle this!" I practically yelled as I ran out my door and down the hall. "I'm mature, I'm an adult, I can handle this! I'm mature, I'm an adult, I can handle this!"

I was lucky that day: No one saw the crazy girl sprinting down the hall toward the garbage can, yelling, "I'm mature, I'm an adult, I can handle this!" and waving around a coconut full of larvae. No one heard her screech, "I'm mature, I'm an adult, I can handle this!" as she threw the ball of bugs into the garbage can like it was a glob of molten lava. No one listened to her mumble, "I'm mature, I'm an adult, I can handle this," as she used wet paper towels to scrape a layer of slime from her desk drawer.

That, however, was the point. I'd done it myself.

The experience taught me more than just to never leave a fresh coconut unattended. Taking on that swarm of squirming and crawling and flying bugs by myself—and living through it—made me realize that maybe I *was* mature. Maybe I *was* an adult. Most important, whatever it was, maybe I *could* handle it. I'm not saying that nothing ever scared me again, but when you've dealt with something that gross, the rest of life's little emergencies tend to fall into a very comforting perspective.

ALAINA SMITH

Choice is one cleanser, clarity is another.
IYANLA VANZANT

THE DIFFERENCE OF
TEN YEARS

*I*recently attended my ten-year high school reunion
and found it to be a shockingly wonderful experience. I
hated high school while I attended it. I was smart and
not really popular in any way, though I was spared the incessant
teasing reserved for some. I had a small group of friends, but I
never felt that I truly fit in, and I was unhappy most of the time
that I was there.

What an eye-opening experience I had at my ten-year reunion
when, instead of rushing by everyone in the hall and making
eye contact with only the few that I knew would acknowledge my
existence, I actually sat down and really talked to people. Instead
of assuming that they were all criticizing me or that I could know
all by observing, I talked to everyone: the popular, the unpopular,
the bad boys, the snotty girls. I found out such amazing things.

I learned that while I had a long-standing reputation as a goody
two shoes, people never thought as badly of me as I did of myself.

I learned that the really cute, popular girls didn't feel that they
were half as wonderful as I had always perceived them to be.

I learned that the guy who I adored who broke my heart because he didn't adore me wasn't the kind of person I wanted to be with anyway.

I learned that the cute sexy captain of the football team who I thought ignored me when I smiled at him in the hall was actually suffering from concussions most of the time and probably never even saw me. Turns out he felt as lonely and unhappy and full of angst as I did in high school.

I learned that the girls from the volleyball team would probably have been better friends to me than the ones that I chose.

I learned that the unattractive girl who everyone teased and laughed at became a beautiful and accomplished woman that they didn't even recognize.

I learned that the most popular girl who was so mean to me for no reason turned into an unhappily divorced woman who lives in the same town we grew up in.

I learned that the kid who seemed headed nowhere at sixteen could grow up into a wonderful husband, father, and successful businessman.

I learned that ten years can make all the difference in the world when you want to learn a little perspective.

I learned that who I have become has more to do with who I am and what I think of myself than what anyone from my high school ever thought of me.

I wish that when I was unhappy or discouraged in high school I would have taken a moment to look beyond that world and say to myself: *I wonder if this will matter to me in ten years.* I am thrilled to say that not a lot of it does.

SUSAN LAMAIRE

ONCE UPON A TIME

My wedding day began at 4 A.M. at Disney World. I had my hair and makeup done, and my mother met me with tea and a camera. She helped me into my dress and fastened the delicate, satin buttons up the back of the heavily laced bodice. I twirled for her in front of the mirror while we both shared a special moment together. By 6 A.M. we were at a nearby park to have the bride photos taken. The wedding ceremony was still more than four hours away.

The day felt surreal when we met up with the bridesmaids. They looked gorgeous in their off-the-shoulder royal blue silk dresses. Several hours later, a limo arrived to whisk them and my mother off to the rose garden at the Yacht Club where the ceremony would take place.

The tension I'd felt earlier melted away. Everything was falling into place. My hair stylist found a solution to my unwieldy veil: Once the photographs were taken, she replaced it with a tiara. I was sure about the wonderful man I'd said yes to, and I wasn't nervous about the wedding itself, even though all eyes would be plastered on me. The only thing that had me a little worried was the possibility that I'd spill something large and obnoxious on my dress.

Just before 10 A.M., Melissa, the wedding coordinator, met me in the hotel lobby to tell me the coach was coming. She informed me we would be starting a bit late because the photographer had just finished up with the groom and groomsmen. She assured me that the guests had arrived and everything was going smoothly.

That's when I looked outdoors to see people on the curb in front of the hotel turn and point. Standing on my tiptoes, I caught a glimpse of the coach coming around on the boardwalk.

"It's time," Melissa's assistant said. She smiled and ushered me outside and down the stairs toward the street. I was surprised with the onslaught of flash bulbs, stares, and smiles from strangers and little girls waving at me.

For a moment, I felt ridiculous. It hadn't occurred to me in all the planning that I would be walking out to climb into Cinderella's coach, dressed like a princess, at Disney World, all by myself. But that's exactly what I did. I couldn't help but smile as I waved at the little girls who were excitedly jumping up and down. The little boys were more interested in the four white horses pulling the carriage and the white-wigged coachmen and driver.

The driver helped me up into the carriage. As I found a way to settle myself, bouncy layers of taffeta underneath my dress spilling everywhere, I saw one little girl staring at me with such earnest wonder in her eyes. Something tugged inside my heart. For me this was my wedding day, a day of discomfort in a dress, and a day when I would join my life to another. For the little girl gazing at me outside the coach, it was a fairy tale come to life with a princess, horses, and a carriage.

"This is it," said the coach coordinator. "If you want to bail, we can have you out of here in ten minutes."

"Excuse me?" I blinked and stared at him. The driver leaned toward me and nodded. "Some brides get jittery and change their minds."

Wow.

"Do brides really do that?" I blurted out while sitting in my five hundred dollar wedding dress, feeling every bit of the corset digging into my ribs and desperately wishing that I'd elected to get married in shorts and tennis shoes.

"Some brides do," he answered, smiling at me. "I just wanted you to know that if you wanted to, we can take care of that, too."

The hilarity of the offer made me laugh. We'd flown family and friends here to be with us. Did I want to bail on the wedding we'd been planning for months?

Not bloody likely!

I looked over at the little girl once again. Her eyes were shining.

I will never forget her face for as long as I live, because in her eyes I saw all the promise of the day ahead of me. No matter how hard I laughed during the ceremony or how relieved I was when I was finally out of the dress and into something comfortable again, the little girl with her dreams of glass slippers and a prince in a castle will forever mark the day I was married.

"No, I'm not going to bail," I told the coordinator. "I've been looking forward to this day since I was a little girl."

He smiled and nodded, then talked into his radio. We were up. It was time for our grand entrance at the Yacht Club. I heard the driver cluck to the horses and we were off with a clippity-clop to make a dream come true.

HEATHER V. LONG

You must do the thing you think you cannot do.
ELEANOR ROOSEVELT

SPEAKING TRAUMAS

During *my junior year of high school, the coun-selor* pulled me aside with this startling news: If I kept my grades up, I would be the salutatorian of my grad-uating class.

The news produced elation, some confusion, and finally, ter-ror. Didn't salutatorians have to give speeches? Cold moisture gathered on my palms, and my heart pumped out a sick death march.

I was expected to give a speech? I was the girl who nearly fainted in the fifth grade while doing a one-minute book report. Before an audience, my voice always trembled, I always spoke too fast, and I could hardly meet anyone's eyes. Putting me behind a podium was akin to sliding my neck through a noose for public execution.

I hated the scrutiny of audiences. I enjoyed talking to people on an individual basis and small groups were fine, but to stand before all those judgmental gazes was terrifying. I was sure they would discover all my flaws. I was certain that I wouldn't measure up. I would be a failure in their eyes.

Since education had always been my refuge, the opportunity to discover what was good and worthy inside myself, I turned once more to learning. I decided to enroll myself in a speech class during my senior year.

I knew I would hate the experience, but it was my only opportunity for change. Only excessive practice would prepare me for that all-important night. I envisioned a whole year of knee-knocking, clammy palms, and blushes, and my stomach twisted. When I walked to class that first day, I felt like an inmate walking down death row, facing a slow and painful end.

And that first semester of speech class was a kind of death. I was forced to put aside my fears, step up to the podium, and make a fool of myself while I fumbled around for confidence. I said some stupid things, made wild gestures, forgot my lines, and felt my body shaking uncontrollably at times. I guess you could call it a phobia, but I didn't want to be its victim. I wanted to slay the dragon, even though it meant walking through the fire.

The end of the school year finally arrived. For my project, I had to give an instructional speech, so I taught the class how to make paper airplanes. Surprisingly, when I turned to face the class, I no longer felt the terror. Maybe a brief moment of misgiving and then it was gone. I completed my presentation after twenty minutes and then listened to my classmates' feedback.

"You're just so different now," an athletic junior, who always seemed to overflow with confidence, told me. "At the beginning of the year you were terrified, and now when you do a speech, it's like nothing to you. You just get up there and do it."

His words and the experience soothed my nerves. I could do the graduation speech. I felt prepared and very calm. I wrote the words to my salutatorian address and started practicing the words over and over and over again. I must have said the speech about fifty times in my room, in the bathroom before the mirror, and in my head. The words came out glibly, smoothly, and professionally. I could do this.

But when graduation night arrived, excitement, fear, nervousness, and dread threatened my confidence. My head knew I could do the speech, but my emotions weren't cooperating. On edge, I practiced the speech about a dozen more times and prayed for God's help and guidance. This event was so important to so many people. What if I failed?

In the middle of practicing my speech, I went downstairs to the kitchen for a break. My relatives had gathered together for my special night. Tense, I sat down in a chair and inhaled the aroma of cooking food.

"Why don't you practice your speech in front of us?" one of my relatives suggested.

The fear sprang back to life. I just wanted a break from the speech, and the thought of performing before family made me even more nervous.

"I don't want to," I said edgily. "I've been practicing all day."

My relative became agitated. She knew about my shyness, which had haunted me all my life. Although she was not a cruel person, she had a habit of throwing out words in an emotional moment, naïvely unaware of their power and impact. Afraid I would embarrass the family, she said with conviction, "You'll be the worst speaker there."

The words tore at my confidence and lodged in my heart. I stumbled upstairs, locked myself in the bathroom, and cried, thinking about her negative remarks. When my tears were gone, I stared at my red eyes and running nose, feeling very pathetic and small. If my relative, whom I loved and trusted, didn't believe in me, how could I believe in myself? And how could any of those strangers believe in me, either?

I washed my face, tried to cover the damage with make-up, and prayed to God for strength and courage. I was still angry and upset, but gradually a sense of duty and purpose overtook my emotions. I wouldn't let anyone down. I would give the speech, despite how I felt.

Hours later, my classmates and I marched to "Pomp and Cir-cumstance" while we took our seats for the ceremony. As we marched, I looked around at the beaming, relieved faces of our friends and family and felt my own smile surface in return. This was it! We were finally going to graduate from high school!

Because I was giving the salutatorian address, I marched up to the stage and took my seat there, waiting for my name to be called. Although I was a little nervous, I felt prepared. I felt strong. I was so proud of my classmates, and I wanted to share this wonderful moment with them.

And a funny thing happened as they called my name and I stepped up to that podium. I wasn't afraid! I took the microphone, and as I talked, my usually soft-spoken voice sounded loud and powerful. The audience was staring at me, but instead of feeling intimidated, I felt honored to address them. I caught the eye of a father holding his toddler, and the child waved at me. I smiled, encouraged by the gesture, and continued through my speech.

When I was finished, hundreds of clapping hands greeted my ears. I had never felt so much joyous emotion directed my way. I floated on that sound, as if all those hands were holding up my poor, tired soul. It had been a long journey, but in that moment, feeling connected with all those people, I knew it had been worthwhile.

KATHLEEN STURGEON

GOING DUTCH

"**A**lways pay for yourself and you'll have a say about where you're going and what you're doing," my mother repeated throughout my teenage years.

And she put her money—her hard earned money, I must say—where her mouth was. As early as twelve, when I went with my neighbor Ray to the movies, she tucked money in my pocket, whispering, "You owe him nothing." I knew she knew how absurd her suggestion was in the context of Ray's painful shyness. He never spoke to anyone but me; he'd die before trying anything inappropriate. But my mother was not one to miss a chance to teach me about life.

My father was a lawyer to the poor and my mother an executive secretary to the rich. Together they kept us comfortable in our spacious rented apartment, but were never able to materialize the dream of actually owning a home of equal size.

My mother's practical streak was of the frugal kind: A new sweater should last three winters and still look new when handed down to my cousin. She wouldn't invest in a piano until I had proven my virtuosity with one hand on the accordion. (Sure enough, I failed the one-hand test.) My parents' one luxury was an every-other-summer trip to Europe, a month-long ship-and-train voyage that culminated with a visit to my father's sister in Switzerland.

I always had boyfriends, and the line between going out for ice cream as a buddy or a date was set in my mind by my paying my share. The boys' hormone-clogged teenage brains, too hazy for the mysteries of girls' periods and giggled secrets, met my going Dutch with the same confusion reserved for all things female.

At fourteen, I was physically underdeveloped and solemn, yet pretty enough to draw the attention of much older boys. When they asked me to restaurants and discos, my mother insisted I go Dutch even though the places were out of my parents' league. I always left the house with a lot more money than I needed. "Just in case," my mother would say. The boys' reactions to my paying varied from a feeble protest to a surprised acceptance. But there was never unwanted heavy panting in cars or forced goodbye kisses in the lobby of my building.

When for my sixteenth birthday my boyfriend gave me a simple watch, my mother insisted the gift was too "meaningful" and I should return it. I lost my fight with her and returned the watch.

The issue of my "independence" was put aside for the rest of my high school years when I dated Danny, who was my age and manifested the charming combination of limited financial resources and expensive taste when picking concerts and comedy clubs. Our sharing expenses down to the penny became as routine as Danny's acceptable gifts of single roses and Swiss chocolate.

I was often embroiled in heated debates with my girlfriends. "If a guy wants my company, he should pay for it," they argued unanimously.

"Why go there?" I argued back. "If a guy pays, it sets up an expectation that you owe him something."

But when in college I attracted the occasional attention of a rich guy, my girlfriends pointed out that it was ridiculous for me to try matching his wallet while it also fell on me alone to invest in clothes and grooming.

"You want equality and then you throw it out the window the moment a guy shows up," I replied. "Principle is principle."

But even I had a moment's hesitation when an heir to one of the world's largest cigarette manufacturers took me out to a restaurant where my half of the dinner was close to my mother's weekly salary. I offered to pay with the same vehemence I always had.

Since paying my college expenses stretched my parents' resources to the limit, I crammed four years into three in order to get out into the world and gain financial independence. I assumed a load of twenty-four credits a semester, but had to skip most mass lectures so I could work as a well-paid three-language translator. And while I did my own hair, nails, and waxing, my mother and I spent my school breaks buying fabrics on sale and cutting three dresses at a time. We would add sleeves to the floral one, a scooped collar to the polka-dot one, and pockets to the plaid one.

Before settling down with the next boyfriend, other occasional "heirs" appeared during my single life. One from an oil refinery, one a candy conglomerate, and another a hotel chain. Even though I was serious, guileless, and not flirtatious, they sought out my company. Maybe they were relieved that I was unimpressed with their money and they found my reaction to the person, not the family ties, refreshing.

At the end, the "Dutching" principle gave me a say in everything I wanted to do. Yet, by paying for myself and expecting no preferential treatment because of my gender, I had to be selective; I couldn't afford the jerks, the narcissists, and the bores. What did interest me were the out-of-the-ordinary studies or work, which resulted in my spending time with them at a physics lab, a radio station, an architectural drafting department, and the bowels of a navy destroyer.

Best of all, with no strings attached, I regarded myself as a true equal. This conviction zapped my male friends with a new kind of respect for me, because in my way, I showed my respect to them.

TALIA CARNER

Only that which is deeply felt can change us.
MARILYN FERGUSON

DARING TO WEAR THE GLASS SLIPPER

D uring high school, I worked at a bridal shop. I loved
the dresses we sold—especially the prom dresses—and
I loved trying them on and pretending that I was someone else. I imagined showing up at my senior prom in one of
those gorgeous dresses and surprising everyone by being absolutely breathtaking.

But I wasn't a daring, slinky-dress-wearing movie star. I was
a shy, quiet high school girl. I was one of those girls who could be
in your history class all year and you'd never even notice.

With my friends, though, I was different. I was talkative and
silly. Only a few people knew that—only those few who had managed to get past my shy exterior.

Even my friends who knew me best were surprised by what I
did my senior year.

I had a hard time selecting a dress for the prom. I watched as
other girls my age came to the bridal shop and picked out their
dresses and their shoes and their matching jewelry. I helped
my friends pick out their dresses, giggling as they sashayed in
front of the full-length mirror. But when they asked me what I
was wearing to the prom, I didn't have an answer.

Actually, I already had my favorite dress picked out, but I wasn't daring enough to wear it. I tried it on often, pretending that it was mine, but I just couldn't wear it in public. What would everyone say? I'd probably just look silly and get laughed out of my own senior prom.

Yet, I loved that dress. It was perfect. It was the *real* me—fun and a little crazy. And that was exactly why I couldn't buy it. It was black and white with a strapless black sequin-covered top and a full white skirt that was mid-thigh in the front and long in the back. It looked like something out of a music video, and I loved it. But I just didn't dare . . .

One day, however, in a burst of courage—and with enough prodding by my coworkers, who had seen me in the dress half a million times—I decided to go for it. What convinced me to buy that dress, I don't know. Maybe it was the fact that I'd be graduating soon, which meant that I'd only have to deal with the ridicule for a month before I escaped to college. Or maybe I just wanted to be a little bit daring—just once.

Every time I thought about the upcoming prom, I got excited. But mostly, I just got nervous. Whenever I talked about my dress, I talked about it with a nervous giggle. I couldn't believe that the dress was mine—and that I was really going to wear it in front of my whole school. I wondered if I could really do it.

Finally, the Big Day came. I got out of school early on that Friday afternoon so I could get my hair done. When I told my hairdresser about my dress (with a nervous giggle), she suggested doing something different with my hair—to match my dress. She spent hours curling my long, thick blonde hair. Then she pinned the top layer of curls to the top of my head, letting them cascade down. When I looked in the mirror, I giggled even more. I loved it.

I drove home shaking excitedly. As I opened the door to the house, I called, "You might want to sit down!" (I remember entering the house the same way a few years later, when the same hairstylist dyed my blonde hair dark red.) When I walked inside, my mom was shocked. I think her jaw may have hit the ground. I giggled again with excitement as I ran off to get into my dress.

Once I was ready, Mom took her standard roll of pictures. And when my date showed up, she took another roll. As I climbed into the car and waved to my parents, I realized that I wasn't really nervous anymore. I was just excited—excited to show off the real me.

I had such a great time that night. I still have stacks of pictures of myself—all with a huge, confident grin that I'd never had before. I loved the attention I got that night. I loved the surprised looks and I especially loved how the guys' looks often said, "Why didn't I notice her before?" I felt like Cinderella.

I honestly believe that my prom dress opened something in me. It made me realize that maybe I wasn't so bad after all. It gave me the boost of confidence that I needed to break out of my shell. By my five-year class reunion, I was an entirely different person. I wore what I wanted—and I did it with a smile. And as I talked to a classmate at that reunion, I beamed with pride as he said, "I just remember you wore *that dress* to the prom . . ."

KRISTIN DREYER KRAMER

THE ADONIS

"*I don't feel right about this. Should we turn around?*" my fifteen-year-old friend Kelly asked.

"No way!" I walked farther down the beach. Somewhere among the dunes a reggae band was jamming. "It'll be okay. We'll just check out the band and leave. No one even needs to know," I assured her.

Moving closer, we discovered a waterfront hotel bursting with college students. They were hanging out in the open-door rooms, on the steps up to the balconies, and filling the entire parking lot all the way down to the beach. From the roof the calypso rhythm drifted down. How intriguing the world of older people can be!

On the sandy beach underneath the awnings of the hotel's pavilion, tanned college-age girls danced in skimpy bikinis. Guys in swim trunks lined up near the kegs and hung out below the neon hotel sign. Some of them had beers in their hands; others were smoking what looked like cigarettes but smelled really acrid. To us, two young teens, this scene opened up a whole new exciting world we'd never seen before.

I knew my mother wouldn't be happy if she knew we were checking out a college party with these activities going on. Still, a part of me wanted to be part of the alluring action. I was almost an adult. After all, I was already fifteen.

"Look at all these guys! They're gorgeous!" Kelly announced. "Check out the one in the yellow trunks."

My eyes scanned the crowd and found the one she was talking about. *An Adonis*, I thought to myself. The Goddess Aphrodite herself couldn't have ignored a man this handsome. Blond sun-streaked hair, evenly tanned skin, and a tall, muscular body—what a hunk he was, I decided.

"He's staring straight at us," Kelly gasped.

She was right. I was so busy admiring his incredible body that I didn't realize he had removed his shades and placed them on top of his head. His eyes beamed blue like the ocean, his teeth glistened against his sun-kissed face.

"He's got to be a model!" I concluded.

Suddenly the band stopped, but the crowd began chanting, "More! More! More!"

I hardly noticed the reggae music restarting. My stomach began churning and my head pounded because this gorgeous guy was snaking toward us through the crowd of gyrating dancers.

Kelly said in my ear, "Be cool."

How could I be cool? I thought I was going to be sick from nervousness.

"Hi," the Adonis said to me. "My name's Hardy. What's yours?"

"Mi—Shelly. Everyone calls me Shelly." *Why didn't I confess my name was Michele?*

"Well, hi, Shelly," he grinned. "Would you like a beer?" He handed me a plastic cup filled with booze.

One drink couldn't hurt, I thought. Eager to please him, I placed the plastic to my lips. "Sure. Thanks."

Suddenly Kelly grabbed the cup from my hand and shoved it back into his chest, spilling some across his well-defined stomach. "We don't drink."

I could have screamed. That was rude. Hardy was only trying to make conversation.

"I wanted to invite you to hang out with me at my beach house down the street, Shelly." He wiped his belly. "But I guess you don't know how to party."

"Your beach house sounds like fun," I said.

"We're late meeting our boyfriends," Kelly interrupted.

Before I could even tell Hardy I didn't have a boyfriend, he had disappeared back into the crowd.

"Hardy!" I called out, searching through the dancers.

Like a dream, he had vanished.

Outraged, I turned to Kelly. "Why did you tell him I had a boyfriend?" I asked her. "Why did you lie?"

"He doesn't know your age. He thinks you're older. Best to be careful," she warned.

"I can't believe you!" I shouted. "Hardy was hitting on me!"

"Come on. Let's go," Kelly responded, grabbing my arm.

All the way back to her house, I didn't talk to her. I couldn't believe she had blown my chances. He could have been The One. He could have been Mr. Right. He was Mr. Right! He was so incredibly handsome . . . and he was talking to me!

"Are you mad at me?" Kelly asked as my mom drove up.

Without looking back, I got in the car and left.

Days passed. On Wednesday morning the phone rang. I saw on Caller ID that it was Kelly's number. Still angry, I wasn't sure if I wanted to pick up the phone. With friends like her who needs enemies? What if she did this for the rest of my life? I'd never have a date if she kept telling every new hunk that I already had a boyfriend.

The answering machine picked up. "Michele, look at section D of the paper this morning. Call me back." Kelly hung up.

Reluctantly, I picked up the newspaper on the coffee table, wondering why she wanted me to look. I flipped through the pages until I got to section D. There was a picture of Hardy right on the front page. Kicking a soccer ball, he looked like a pro in his yellow shirt and loose black shorts. Glancing down from the picture, I read the headline. LOCAL SOCCER STAR ARRESTED. I quickly read on.

"Soccer player accused of using drug to brutally beat and rape a fifteen-year-old girl. Released from the hospital, the teen picked the player out of a police lineup. After obtaining a search warrant, the police discovered a bottle of the drug nicknamed 'Roofie' in his apartment along with the fifteen-year-old's half-carat diamond pendant. This is the second time this star's been accused," the article continued. "On another similar occasion . . ."

I dropped the paper and stumbled to the phone, trembling. That could have been me! That could have been me in that apartment getting raped, even beaten.

When Kelly answered, I apologized. Luckily, she forgave me for avoiding her the last couple of days and was glad she had stopped me from drinking from that plastic cup at the hotel.

I thanked her countless times.

From this experience I learned more than don't accept anything from strangers. I now know to listen to my head and not my hormones. My life is far too precious to risk over any pretty face—even an Adonis.

MICHELE WALLACE CAMPANELLI

ONE FINE DAY

When I first heard the anonymous quote, "Love like you have never been hurt" in my early teens I had no idea what it meant. I loved my family and had never been hurt by them; I loved my friends and had never been hurt by them. Whoever said this quote must not know what they are talking about. How could love hurt me?

During my senior year in high school, I finally found out what it means to "Love like you have never been hurt." I had been dating Brad for almost three months. It started out like the typical high school relationship, talking on the phone constantly. He attended another school so we spent time together on the weekends and tried to watch each other's after-school activities as often as possible.

Then Brad started to act really strange around me. I couldn't figure out why. One night, not long after, he told me it was over between us because his friend Brandon did not approve of the relationship. *How can that be? Didn't Brandon want Brad to be happy?* Brad's other friends told me how happy I had made him and that they wouldn't get rid of me for anything. *So why Brandon? What did I do to him to make him hurt me like this?* After a couple of weeks of desperately missing Brad, Brandon called me to say how sorry he was. He never meant to hurt either of us. He had felt that I was taking his place as Brad's best friend. He felt so badly that he helped Brad set up my dream date to bring us back together.

On date night I was told to fix my hair and make-up like I was attending a prom, but not to dress up. Brandon called and asked me to go to Brad's house. (I learned later that Brad's parents were clued in and they'd left the front door unlocked.) As soon as I opened the door, I followed the candles to a box with a rose on it. I took the lid off and under the tissue was a gorgeous long black dress with a pair of shoes to match. I put the dress on, then heard a honk from outside. I looked out the window and saw a hunter green mustang waiting for me. (Brad had rented it for our date because it was my dream car.) I walked up to the car and looked in. Instead of seeing Brad, Brandon was in the driver's seat wearing jeans and a sweatshirt. *What is going on?* I got in and Brandon apologized again for messing up my relationship with Brad. He wouldn't tell me anything more. We drove to the Eagle's Nest restaurant in Indianapolis. My favorite place! Brandon said he would make sure my car made it home and not to worry about anything. Everything was just the way it should be.

When I entered the lobby, the waiter led me to a table where Brad was waiting with a bouquet of roses. The rest of the night was pure magic, a carriage ride, dancing, and even the song. We talked openly about what had happened between us. When he took me home, he serenaded me with the tune by 98° called "I Do." He ended the evening by telling me how much he loved me. I didn't know what to say. I really cared for him, but was it "love"? I went inside and thought it over a million times that night.

The next morning I awoke to the feeling of being loved and knowing I loved this man back. I couldn't wait to tell him! He was coming to watch me photograph a wrestling match that night, so I could tell him then how I felt and let the magic be complete.

I could hardly sit still in the gym while I was taking pictures. I couldn't wait for him to show up. But he never did. I waited and waited for hours, but he never came. No one was home at his house, and he wasn't returning my pages. All I could think was that he was hurt.

Around midnight that night, I received a phone call from his mother. She was crying so hard that she couldn't speak. His dad took the phone and I heard it; I heard the hurt. When Brad was on his way to see me, he had been hit by a drunk driver and killed instantly. The hurt filled my body from head to toe. I never got to tell him I loved him. I never got to say goodbye. The hurt took over my life for months to come. I frequently found myself asking God why this had to happen.

Then, out of nowhere, I heard that saying again, "Love like you have never been hurt." It hit me like a ton of bricks because I finally knew what it meant. Brad had meant the world to me and I will always love him. After all, he was my first love. I have become a better person because of him. I realize that life is full of good times and bad, but each is used to help make me a stronger person than I was before. Loving Brad was a very good time in my life. Love allowed me to see hope in all that is good and all that has the potential to be good. Losing him was a bad time, but it taught me that when you love someone as much as I did Brad, then you have the potential to love other people just that much more. Suddenly, the hurt did not feel the same anymore. My hurt had been replaced by hope. Hope that—one fine day—I truly may love again like I have never been hurt.

DANIELLE ARMITAGE

III
FITS AND STARTS

*There is no way to feel fully alive
unless you are willing to start your day
with at least one optimistic option.*

JENNIFER JAMES

MIMEO MADNESS

*L*ooking back to my junior high school years from the distance of adulthood, I'm sure there were times when the other kids in my class would have loved to clobber me. I won most spelling bees, I made straight A's, and I was president of the student council. While I didn't sneak behind the janitor's shed to smoke with the leather jacket crowd, I did have a charcoal circle skirt with pink felt poodles glued on it. And my mother bought me a white, cotton, circle-stitched, pointy-cupped Maidenform bra, even though I needed it less than many of the other girls. I stuffed it with my father's handkerchiefs and wore it proudly.

As eighth grade began, the same kids from the previous year plus several new ones sat in the long rows of desks facing the blackboard. In the fifties, the cornfields of Kansas crowded right up to the windows along one side of our cinder block school, but the dust of backhoes digging basements for yet another tract of suburban houses clouded the horizon.

Mrs. Hagan, our teacher, ruled from the front of the class in her straight skirts and sensible cardigans. Her helmet of gunmetal gray hair shone as lectured us in a gravelly voice, supervising our reading of *Great Expectations*. Then she announced a test for the next day.

Everyone groaned. A test the first week of school? Who had ever heard of such a thing?

The following morning, Mrs. Hagan rushed late into class. Many sighed with relief when she announced the test would be delayed as she hadn't had time to mimeograph it and, "I can't leave the classroom unattended in order to do it now."

But I seethed. I had missed *The Art Linkletter Show* in order to study, and the information needed to pass the test bubbled at the front of my mind.

Never giving a thought to how the rest of the students might feel, I offered to take the test to the supply room behind the principal's office and run the copies off on the mimeograph machine.

She looked at me in amazement and then agreed.

Clutching the sticky reverse-image master copy in my hand, I hurried out of the classroom, down the long hall, and into the principal's office. His skinny secretary accepted my hall pass with a suspicious stare and nodded me toward the supply room with a jerk of her head that set her corkscrew curls all a-bobble.

The sacred mimeo machine stood in the corner, and the wet, inky, chemical smell clung to the entire room. Positioning the master copy into the brackets, I began turning the handle. As the roller spun in clackety circles, the rattling of the printing process cut off the whisper of fresh paper being whisked from the stack. Wanting to get the thirty-six copies made as quickly as possible, I cranked the handle faster and faster. The copies piled up at the right side of the machine, immediately curling at both ends like gift wrap off a roll.

In the hypnotic rhythm of the whirling machine, I lost track of how many I had completed, and I stopped to count. The slick, seaweedlike feel of the cold, damp copies between my fingers enchanted me. Nothing could have stopped me from raising the stack of damp tests to my face and inhaling the heady aroma from the center of the roll.

Nirvana!

Eyes closed in an aromatic trance, I was startled by the prissy office clerk's voice.

"What on earth do you think you're doing, young lady?" She stood in the doorway with her arms folded across her chest. She couldn't have looked more shocked if she'd caught me smoking with the teachers.

"I just need to count these . . ." I mumbled, yanking my hands down from my face and counting the copies with sweaty finger-tips. She glared at me as I made eleven more spins of the handle and escaped back to the classroom.

Only Mrs. Hagan smiled when I returned. Most of the students refused to meet my eyes. A girl in the front row divided the test copies into six piles, one for each row of desks, and hand-over-hand we passed them to the back of the room. Soon everyone bent to the task, and the room was very quiet.

I finished the test, walked to the front of the class, and laid my exam on the corner of Mrs. Hagan's desk. As I returned to my seat, a few of my classmates glanced at me. Their initial looks of resentment changed to amusement, and they ducked their heads and twitched their mouths. A suppressed wave of giggles rolled up the aisle behind me.

It wasn't until I went into the girls' bathroom two hours later that I discovered the source of their mirth. As I inhaled the per-fume of the freshly mimeographed papers, pressing them to my face in near ecstasy, ink from the wet copies had transferred to my face. In mirror image, I could read whole words on my goody two shoes, blushing, thirteen-year-old face.

PEGGY VINCENT

LESSONS FROM
THE SCHOOL NURSE

As a junior, I cut classes and hung with a rough crowd. I knew I didn't belong with these kids, but they were the most accepting of the cliques. It didn't take long for the vice-principal to catch up with me and my antics. I'd get "busted" and assigned to detention. Detention never deterred me much—I got attention through punishment. When detention failed, in-school suspension was the next step. No problem. Getting an "in-school" was an even bigger attention grabber.

My parents were at their wits' end with me. While my older brother was their shining star, I caused them considerable embarrassment and shame as their problem child.

The teachers would shake their heads. "Why can't you be more like your brother? He was a joy to have in class."

Their questions tore through my heart, fueling my rebellious attitude. I responded with a belligerent shoulder shrug. I hated school. Sometimes I think school hated me, too.

In mid-September, I met with my guidance counselor to drop an elective art class. I signed up for the class because my "friends" claimed they had, too. I was furious when I saw none of them on the roster. The counselor agreed to the drop, but told me I had to make a choice. I had to choose between being a helper in the nurse's office or working in the main office. My mind, always searching for the path of least resistance, figured I could get away with more by heading for the nurse's office.

The next day, I strolled into my new assignment and flopped

my books on the chair in the waiting room. Seated at her desk, Mrs. Grey looked at me over the top of her half glasses.

"Books don't belong on chairs. People belong on chairs."

"And I should put them where exactly?" I inquired, my head cocked to one side, hands defiantly on my hips.

"Anywhere but there. I have a job for you, so wash your hands with hot water and plenty of soap," she said, sizing me up.

I begrudgingly complied. Normally, I would have spouted off a smart-aleck response. But there was something different about her—something in her tone and those piercing blue eyes that told me she wouldn't stand for it and she had zero tolerance for my attitude.

She led me to a room hidden in the back of her office. The brightly-lit space had a commode and a sink, some storage cabinets, a countertop workspace, and a small refrigerator. Mrs. Grey darted around the tiny room with meticulous accuracy, demonstrating the procedure for using a color-changing test strip to check pH levels in a urine sample.

"Wait a minute," I said, my hands returning to my hips. "You expect me to put a dip stick in all those containers of pee?" I was horrified by the thought. There were more than a hundred urine samples in her little fridge.

"Not all at once," she replied with a raised eyebrow. "That wouldn't be very accurate now, would it?"

Reluctantly, I set to work on the little plastic bottles. The samples were required for the upcoming winter sports teams. I felt I was learning a lot more about my classmates than I really wanted to know.

The job wasn't as bad as I thought. Mrs. Grey looked on approvingly as I worked. She complimented my carefulness and how quickly I learned. It was the first time a school official approved of something I was doing—a far cry from the exasperated expressions I received from the teachers.

When the bell rang for the next class period, I was sorry to have to leave the safety of the health office and the approval of my new friend and mentor. I looked forward to the next day's visit.

Without fully realizing it, I began counting on Mrs. Grey more and more for help and advice. One warm Friday afternoon in October, we chatted about the upcoming weekend.

"Do you have any big plans for the break?" I asked.

"Well, my daughter's coming home from college. I thought maybe she and I would go and see that new dance movie that just came out. I hear the music is fantastic!" she answered, swaying her hips and snapping her fingers.

"Sounds like fun." I looked at the floor.

She stopped dancing and studied me. "How about you? Any plans?"

"Oh, I dunno," I responded, hesitantly.

She gave me her now familiar look that said, "Okay, what gives?"

"Well," I stammered, "there's this party at Branson's field. It sounds so cool. Everybody's going."

"Ah, a field party. And," she continued, "will there be drinking at this field party?"

"Probably. But I really want to go. Joey will be there and I've liked him for so long! It would be the perfect time to hang out with him, ya know, just chillin'."

"Uh-huh."

"And I know I can use my dad's car this weekend. He said so himself."

"Well," she sighed, "you have to follow your own heart, dear. You know right from wrong."

Before she could continue, I already had my answer. Going to a field party would be a mistake. Drinking and driving would be an even bigger mistake. My family was proud of the changes in me— and so was I. My grades were getting better, I wasn't cutting classes, and my parents were showing more trust in me with each passing day. Getting caught at a field party would wipe out all the progress I had made.

"You're right," I said with a sigh.

"Exactly! I'll tell you what. Denise gets home this afternoon, so I thought we'd catch the show at seven. We'll pick you up at six-thirty. Sound like a good plan?"

"Yeah, it sounds like a good plan." I smiled.

"That's my girl!" she sang out and hugged me tight.

Mrs. Grey and I formed a lasting friendship as I worked in her office for the next two years. Her no-nonsense approach, along with her warmth, love, and acceptance gave me a purpose in school. I never looked back for my so-called "friends."

Our trust and friendship went far beyond any adult relationship I ever had, except for my parents. I even had dinner at her house once or twice when I dated her son. Things didn't work out with him, but Mrs. Grey never held it against me. In fact, she never held anything against me, and she never once compared me to my brother. She liked me for who I was and she believed in me. Her belief was all I needed to believe in myself.

Mrs. Grey told me during the last week of my senior year, "You have a bright and wonderful future ahead of you."

Thanks to her efforts, she was right.

BETSY O'BRIEN HARRISON

Memory is the diary we all carry about with us.
MARY H. WALDRIP

CAMP KANAWAUKE

*L*ooking back, I don't know why I wanted to go to summer camp so badly. My older sister and I begged our parents to let us go, and finally they relented after finding an adequate all girls' camp nestled in Bear Mountain in upstate New York. Driving all the way from The Bronx was no easy feat with a thirteen- and fifteen-year-old arguing in the backseat.

This was my first time at camp and my first time so far from home. I was assigned to the "Vikings" group and bunked in a tent. I had an eclectic mix of tent mates. I was sure Heidi, a beautiful blonde girl, would grow up to be a model. Susan was a studious writer who was busily penning a play entitled *Mr. Menstru and the Case of the Ransomed Tampon*. Mary, a quiet girl with very frizzy brown hair that made her look about four inches taller than she really was, and Ellen, the obligatory "girl who is allergic to everything" and who'd be leaving only days later.

My first major catastrophe happened on the very first night. The tent had no screens or netting, and I was experiencing the very high-pitched whine mosquitoes make when they're about to take up residence in your ear canal. Night after night I lay awake plagued by these tiny bastions from hell. They rewarded my animosity by biting me, and I was off to the nurse quite a bit to be slathered with calamine lotion.

The second major catastrophe came on the day we were to take our swim tests. I don't swim. There are no natural bodies of water larger than a bathtub in The Bronx. Because of my inability to swim, I was cast off to the "Crib," a body of water that was sectioned off for the purpose of making kids who can't swim feel like babies.

The Dining Hall provided a safe and comfortable haven away from water and mosquitoes. The counselors (who were about eighteen years old but seemed forty-two) taught us all kinds of songs that made no sense. My favorite of these was a chant that started as a whisper but grew in intensity until everyone was screeching. The words went like this: "Ooh, ka-layla, pera-ticka-temba a muzza, muzza, muzza. Ooh ahh loo ayy ahh loo ahh loo ay." Ah, the wonders of Camp Primal Scream Therapy. Mom and Dad were sure to be proud of my new chanting abilities. There is also something very weird about camp songs—you never, ever forget them. The camp itself had its own song: "There's a camp along Kanawauke shore, Ma-he-tu is its name . . . Rah rah Ma-he-tu rah rah Ma-he-tu . . ." I am convinced that should I meet another alumni of Ma-he-tu, we'd be able to sing every word in unison.

The homesickness I felt the first few days faded away, and I all but forgot I even had parents. I took photos of sunsets with my trusty Kodak camera, found quiet places to sit and read or record my thoughts in a journal, and generally enjoyed camp life. But no camp experience is ever complete without a night (or two) of sheer terror.

Once a week we had something called "vespers," where the different groups would all gather in one tent and the counselor would tell spooky stories. By this time it would be pitch black outside and mighty creepy. Flashlights were produced that we held under our chins, shining up and casting spooky shadows on the faces of the counselors and campers. Of course, this time, the story told was about a hatchet man who lived in the woods and how a couple of campers found the hatchet near their tent, buried deep into the bark of a tree. The story had the desired effect, and as we all went back to our respective tents, my heart was racing. I was convinced this hatchet guy was real and he'd be coming for me (if the mosquitoes didn't get me first). I lay awake that night on constant guard, looking up at the branches of trees and listening to the night sounds of the woods.

The morning light was welcome, and I was soon reminded that it was our tent's turn to clean the latrines. Each tent had to perform different tasks each week, and it wasn't as hard as it sounds—mainly we took the dead bugs out of the sinks and splashed buckets of water on the floors and toilets. They weren't toilets that flushed, just holes that led straight down into darkness.

Camp ended a bit earlier for me than for everyone else, as I was to have a couple more mishaps. When everyone in camp had to take their final swim test, all the groups were brought out onto the docks. We sat in the sun for a couple of hours, and I'd forgotten my sunblock. By the time the tests were over, I had very burned shoulders, arms, and back. I didn't realize how bad it was until that night: I couldn't lie down, much less fall asleep. The next morning I was sent to the infirmary, and my parents were called to come get me. My shoulders and back were blistered and all we could do was apply cold cloths. My parents wouldn't be there until the next morning, so I tried my best to sleep and the nurse set up a small fan to help keep me cool.

I wasn't destined to leave camp without an even bigger to-do, but I wasn't aware of it at the time. That night as I was preparing to go to sleep, the little fan's spinning began to slow. I watched it curiously from my bed as the blades got slower and slower, and finally smoke began pouring out from the motor. I just sat there, completely shocked. As I watched, flames began to lick up out of the motor.

"Uh, nurse?" I screamed, getting out of bed and knocking on her door. "The uh, fan's well, on fire."

The nurse jumped out and ran into the infirmary, grabbed the fan, and brought it outside. A small group of campers and counselors who hadn't yet retired for the evening came to watch the fan burn. What a send-off!

All in all, I think my camp experience was a success. I had a lot of fun and dealt with a few people who didn't like me, a few people I didn't like, a few sticky situations, mutant insects, hatchet men, piranha, and one pretty fun square dance (complete with imported boys!). I learned that if you never take a chance and see what life has to offer, you may save yourself some trouble, but you will also miss all the fun. I had to go out on a limb to learn to stand on my own, and I lived to tell the tale. My experience may not be as intense as winning one million dollars on *Survivor,* but for me at thirteen, wrestling Bear Mountain was enough to prove my mettle.

MAUREEN A. BOTHE

FAMILY CIRCUS

Damsy, my grandmother, screeched to a halt in front of our tiny house, slammed the door of her car, and marched straight into our front room. She was on another mission.

"Waneta, wash the kids' faces and everybody get in the car."

"Mama, what's going on? I'm in the middle of the laundry."

"Well, leave it. The Family Circus is in town for two days, and we *don't* want to miss it."

That's how my grandmother was. If she decided that we were going to do something, we did it in a hurry. So Mom set the washboard aside and let the clothes sit in the boiler of sudsy water. I begrudged going *anywhere* with my family and any other self-respecting twelve-year-old girl felt the same way. But, as usual, I sacrificed myself because the Family Circus was just too hard to resist. In a few minutes, five of us were piling into Damsy's '32 Chevy. Patty, the smallest, climbed onto the little shelf under the back window because she fit there perfectly. Bobby and I sat in the backseat; Damsy drove like a crazy woman, and Mom sat with shoulders sagging, resigned to another surprise outing with our grandmother.

I hated to admit it but Damsy's "outings" were never dull.

Upon arriving at the out-of-town circus we first armed ourselves with plenty of junk food, which was Damsy's treat. Then we strolled past all the sideshows searching for one where children were allowed to buy a ticket if accompanied by an adult. Bobby and I wanted to see the half-man, half-woman exhibit but

Mom said, "Not today, not ever." So we decided to see the two-headed snake exhibit for free. The scaly thing was asleep while we were there but it didn't look like a fake. Through the glass wall Mom inspected the two heads very carefully for any sign of a seam in case it was two snakes stitched together. But she couldn't detect one and declared with satisfaction, "Well, I think this weird thing is for real."

We soon left the sideshow exhibits and found the giant Ferris wheel where Bobby and I were allowed to ride in a seat together. The rest of the family stayed below. Whenever the Ferris wheel stopped to let new people on, we were suspended in midair. It made my stomach tickle and my body sweaty all over, so Bobby rocked the seat on purpose to make me feel even worse. Each time we stopped a little higher in the sky to let another rider aboard, my brother rocked harder than the time before. It scared me to death. I snapped, "Stop that you brat or I'll tell Mom."

My little brother snickered and said in a cold voice, "She can't hear you." We were about ready to go around the highest point of the Ferris wheel when we stopped in midair for one more passenger. There was nothing but sky around me. I was frozen in space and couldn't speak. Bobby watched my face pickle with fear and rocked with all of his might as he laughed like the devil. I was panic stricken and got brave enough to let go of the handle just long enough to wave at my mother one hundred miles below. I screeched, "*Mom! Make him staaahhp!*"

I could barely see her wave a greeting back to me before scampering off to follow Patty. Then Damsy tilted her head way back, shaded her eyes with one hand, and also waved in a friendly manner. She dashed off to follow Mom and my little sister. I thought I would faint and Bobby was so hysterical with laughter that he forgot to rock our seat. I was too frightened to raise my hand again to smack him and he knew it.

That's when I remembered why I hated going places with my family. It always backfired on me. But I had no choice. When

Damsy decided it was time to go for a ride we piled into her car no matter where it might take us. She said that we needed a change of scenery once in a while, but I seriously doubted her judgment.

I felt somewhat recovered from the frightening ride on the giant Ferris wheel until I discovered that our next destination was the Giant Barrel. It was laying on its side, open at both ends and large enough for people to walk through. But the barrel was turning slowly in a clockwise direction as people hopped their way to the opposite end. If they were lucky enough to remain upright after the trip to the other side they jumped out onto a small deck and got a little prize, and I do mean "little." It looked like fun so Damsy said, "Go ahead, try it. My treat."

I went in first, sidestepped easily and made it through partway. That's when I realized that the next section of the barrel was turning in a counterclockwise direction. I hopped onto that part, switched feet, changed my rhythm and made it to the last division of the barrel. But it was turning in a clockwise direction. My body and brain were having trouble getting together, but miraculously I made it through to the other side, repressed a smile, and tried not to show how much I enjoyed it. I wondered how my little brother was doing. After I hopped out onto the deck feeling triumphant I discovered that Bobby had never even started. His arms were hugging his body and I could tell that he was scared.

I hated it when I felt sorry for him.

I saw my mother hand Bobby's ticket to the man and assumed that she was getting a refund. But I was wrong. She was preparing to step into the Giant Barrel herself. I was ashamed. Mothers didn't do things like that. She confidently hopped into the first section of the slowly turning surface and danced her way through the clockwise part, but immediately lost her rhythm in the counterclockwise division. My hands flew to cover my mouth in fear of what might happen next. Was she going to lose her balance?

Yes, she was. My mother was actually falling down in public.

I covered my eyes, peeked through my fingers, and couldn't believe what I was seeing. She rolled up the turning wall and slid back down, up the wall and down the wall. The barrel relentlessly turned and each time, she rolled up and slid back down. Mom tried desperately to regain her footing, but each time she rolled up the wall, which meant rolling back down again. My mother had no control over which way she flopped. She flipped this way, that way, and over there. I was mortified. Her dress was up to her armpits and her bloomers showed. People stopped, alarmed to see a grown woman rolling around in the Giant Barrel.

She yelled at the top of her lungs, "Stop this thing and let me outta here!"

I couldn't breathe. I wanted a different mother; one who would have turned in the ticket for a refund.

I turned away and pretended that I didn't know who she was, but my brother was laughing his head off. The man who operated the machine finally stopped it so my mother could stand up, pull herself together, and stagger out of the Giant Barrel. When she returned to where she had started, my brother was bending over and holding his sides from laughing. Mom snapped, "It's not funny young man!" but Bobby couldn't pull out of it. He was almost crying from cackling. People gathered to make sure my mother was all right while I considered turning myself in for adoption.

As soon as Mom staggered onto solid ground Bobby pranced, clutched his crotch, and said, "I've gotta go to the bathroom." It was growing dark and by that time my mother had to use a toilet as well. But it was too late for Patty. She had already wet her pants. My grandmother threw up her hands and just looked at her eyebrows.

Mom said, "Follow me. We're gonna go behind this tent. No one will see us in the dark. I've got paper napkins."

I was so revolted that I couldn't follow them so Damsy, Patty, and I stayed behind near the lighted promenade and waited. But Mom and my brother were gone for a very long time, and my grandmother was getting worried. I said, "Maybe they got lost." No sooner than I had said it than out of the shadows came my mother, limping, with Bobby holding her purse. Blood trickled from the shinbone of her left leg. My grandmother was alarmed.

"Waneta, what in the Sam Hill happened to you?"

Mom said, "I stumbled over a tent stake." Her voice was tight and she was visibly shaken.

A ragged wound was visible on her leg and blood had dripped all over her shoe. I could tell that it hurt and I wanted to cry. I had been so embarrassed when she rolled up the wall of the Giant Barrel, but now I wanted to hug her and tell her that I was sorry. I looked after my sister while Damsy went to the root beer stand to get ice and paper towels to clean my mother's leg. We helped her hobble to the car and Damsy took us all home. This time she drove carefully. My grandmother spread Mercurochrome into the wound and bandaged it. She then gave my mother two aspirin and said, "Waneta, go to bed."

I felt so sorry for my mom that I lay down beside her until my father came home later that night. I promised myself that first thing in the morning I would work very hard to start liking her again.

BETTY AUCHARD

PASS IT ON

*I*t was a Friday in March when my boyfriend of ten months dumped me. I spent the weekend in my room crying. It wasn't losing that particular guy that upset me so much, because things hadn't been great between us for a while. It was the feeling of rejection and humiliation that drove me to tears. Instead of thinking about ways to win my ex back, I berated myself for not seeing the breakup coming so I could have broken up with him first. "I wish I had been the one to dump him," I sobbed to my stuffed yellow rabbit. "I wish he was the one feeling hurt and unwanted."

By Monday morning, I had stopped crying. I just didn't have the energy to cry any more. Now I felt sick. My eyes were swollen, my head was pounding, and a horrible sore throat practically prevented me from speaking. I was exhausted, but I dragged myself to school. I was sorry I did. Everywhere I went, I saw other couples walking down the hallways together, holding hands or kissing by their lockers. I felt sicker and sicker. I wondered how long it would take until the feeling went away.

The next day, I couldn't get out of bed. Actually, I couldn't even lift my head off the pillow. *He's not going to do this to me,* I thought to myself. *No guy is worth feeling this rotten.* I managed to get down the hall to the bathroom, and I looked at myself in the mirror. What I saw shocked me. I was pale, except for dark circles under my eyes where it looked like someone had punched me. My neck was swollen to the point that a golf ball seemed to be sticking out from each side. Instead of going to school, I went to the doctor.

"I have what?" I asked in shocked disbelief.

"Mononucleosis," my doctor replied.

"That's just my luck," I said to myself. "I get the kissing disease when I'm no longer kissing anyone."

The next few weeks went by in a blur. It hurt to eat. It hurt to move. It hurt to talk. My friends sent me cheery notes and get-well cards, but I was contagious so nobody could come to visit. I didn't even have the energy to talk on the phone. I was miserable. And I was worried.

The prom was coming up, and although the doctor had assured me that I would be fine by then, my prospects weren't looking good. After all, I didn't have a boyfriend anymore, and by the time I got back to school, I figured all the guys would be taken. "The prom is supposed to be the most romantic night of my life," I whined to myself. "And I'll be spending it alone in my room." I couldn't believe how horrible my life had become. *I wish something good would happen to me,* I thought.

Eventually, I felt less exhausted, my head stopped throbbing, and the swelling in my throat went down. I wanted to eat again. And I started thinking about my ex-boyfriend. I wondered if he ever thought about me and if he wanted me back. Most of all, I wondered if he had a date for the prom. I was starting to feel depressed when my phone rang. For the first time in weeks, I answered it.

I'm glad I did. It was my friend, Mike. He asked me how I was feeling and when I would be back in school. I told him that I was much better, I wasn't contagious anymore, and the doctor said I could go back the following week. We talked for a few more minutes, and right before we hung up, he said, "Hey, do you want to go to the prom? You know, as friends." I knew I would have a great time with him. No, it wouldn't be the romantic evening I had dreamed of, but it would be even better: It would be fun. I couldn't say yes fast enough.

I was still smiling when my phone rang again. This time, it was my best friend. "I hear you're going to the prom with Mike," she said. "That'll be great."

I agreed with her and said I couldn't wait, but I also couldn't resist asking about my ex. "Have you seen Bobby around?" I wondered. "Is he seeing anyone? Does he have a date for the prom?"

"I forgot you haven't heard anything for weeks," my friend giggled. "No, Bobby doesn't have a date for the prom. In fact, he won't be going at all."

"Why not?" I asked.

She laughed some more and finally said, "He has mono."

CAROL SJOSTROM MILLER

IN KNEED OF GRATITUDE

I *was born with odd knees. My knees were positioned* just enough out of the socket that they would totally and unexpectedly dislocate. Without any warning, these dislocation "events" occurred at the most surprising and awkward times, leaving me collapsed in a painful heap of immobility. One night it happened as I crossed a busy highway. Enough is enough, my parents decided, and they took me to an orthopedic surgeon. His prognosis was grim. He said I'd spend eight months in a wheelchair after each knee repair. At sixteen years old when a girl should be having fun and kissing, months and months in a wheelchair seemed like forever.

Since we lived only seventy miles from the world-renowned Mayo Clinic, my parents took me there to seek a second opinion. We learned that many European women shared my same knee problem and surgeons there used a different procedure to correct it. The doctor was pleased to offer me the first knee surgery of its kind in the States. How did I handle this opportunity—a possibility to exchange sixteen months in a wheelchair for a few months in walking casts? Like a spoiled brat!

The operations were completed one week apart and were a huge success from a medical standpoint, but I felt supremely sorry for myself. Every one of my three roommates—especially the cheerful woman in her twenties in the bed across from me, six of whose vertebrae had simply disintegrated—made my knee problem seem minor. She was so cheerful it was almost sickening. In contrast, I sulked, complained, and refused to drink fluids, resulting in unnecessary temperature spikes. Soon I gained the notorious reputation among the nurses in the hospital of being the most obnoxious patient.

One day as I lay basking in my gray mood, I looked out the window and noticed strange swirling clouds with green tones painting the horizon. Suddenly a flurry of activity began on the ward: Sirens blared and people shouted, "Tornado!" One of the nurses briskly threw a pillow at me with the abrupt command, "Hurry up. Cover your head!"

If my heart hadn't been pounding out of my chest, I would have laughed hysterically. I was immobile and perched on one of the top floors of the hospital—surrounded by a wall of glass windows as the potential for 200 mile per hour winds headed my way.

Shaking violently, I plugged my ears. I felt like a giant egg waiting to be cracked by shattering glass or worse yet, sucked up like a piece of dust into nature's high-powered vacuum cleaner.

I waited in anticipation and noticed the silence. Everything around me was suspended in time. A minute seemed like an hour. I listened for the train roar, which often accompanies a tornado strike, but I could have heard a pin drop.

After what seemed like eternity, an "all clear" message was announced. The track of the tornado missed the hospital, and we emerged from our covers and pillows to witness another day.

Something happened to me that day—I grew up. The prospect of a tornado taking my life brought me to my senses. While my head was covered under a pillow and my legs were encased in plaster, suddenly I saw my roommate in a new light. I realized her joy was a conscious choice in spite of all she was going through. She was like a teacher to me. Even though she would likely never walk again, her joy in the presence of pain nudged me toward a greater sense of appreciation than I'd ever experienced before. With a choice of being obnoxious or grateful after all the doctors had done for me, I now decided to be grateful.

The following summer, after a full recovery, I strolled to a local beach to expose my scar-decorated knees to the sun. I walked past a boy around my age. He looked at my legs and grunted, "Where did you get those ugly scars on your knees?" Before my surgeries, a comment like this would have shattered my confidence.

My courageous roommate with her cheerful smile flashed into my mind. I faced the boy, did a twirl for him, and proudly modeled the scars on my knees that represented a badge of honor and my switch from being a spoiled brat to a more insightful sixteen-year-old. Then I gracefully walked away—thankful for the life I had been given.

CANDIS FANCHER

A CALCULATED MOVE

I moved my three children to a small southern city from New York in hopes of improving the quality of our lives. This move presented challenges I could not foresee.

My oldest daughter, Rita, was just entering the ninth grade. In my mind, entering the first year of high school was the best time to begin life in a new city. She would be one of many new kids in school. The high school was located in a rural area outside of town, so a seventeen-mile commute was not considered unusual. To my daughter, a city girl, passing cows and farms to get to high school was not a pleasant experience—especially when the fields were being fertilized.

Although Rita complained, I thought she was adjusting. She made new friends, and I let her call her old friends in New York a few times a month. We got through the first year without any major problems.

The following year the school system changed its boundaries and our home was no longer considered in the same district as before. Just as Rita was adjusting, she was expected to change high schools. Understanding the reluctance of students to change high schools, the school officials offered those students who were now considered to be out of their school's area the opportunity to continue attending their present high school if they could provide their own transportation.

Determined to continue at the school where she had friends, Rita arranged to ride with another student who drove to school. I was proud of her. She had been resourceful and found a solution to our transportation problem: There was no way I could figure out how to drive Rita to school, get her two sisters ready for two other schools, and get myself off to work on time. But the friend who drove Rita to school had an old car. The trip back and forth was thirty-four miles and quickly proved to be too stressful for her car. There had to be another way.

In the midst of one of our arguments about school, Rita blurted out that the assistant principal suggested she quit school if it was such a problem to get there. I felt my blood pressure rise as I pictured a school official, an administrator, suggesting to *any* student that he or she drop out of school. I could not understand that kind of thinking. Everyone I knew wanted to encourage students *not* to drop out.

Rita had withheld this information from me for two weeks. She knew I'd fly up to that school and argue with the administrators. But I did not want to do that. I had no interest in talking to people with that kind of mentality, and I did not want my child in a school that was under their guidance. Rita would have to change schools.

Rita was miserable. What I was asking her to do was difficult: to join ranks with those her present classmates considered *the enemy*. She knew only a handful of students from the high school closer to our home. I was asking her to start all over again, just after she was beginning to adjust to our new life in the South.

And, unknown to me at the time, a New York friend of Rita's offered to send her money to leave home if things did not work out.

Rita was shocked at the degree of my response. She expected me to complain, but in a ladylike fashion. I am normally a very quiet person who does not raise her voice. This time I became a wild woman. As the kids would say, I went ballistic! How dare anyone suggest to *my* child that she drop out of school! I yelled and screamed.

I went to the high school closer to our home. Instead of sitting at the counselor's desk and calmly stating my case, I stood in the middle of the main office and ranted and raved about the other school's actions. I told them that I wanted my child to enroll in this school. To calm me down, they were more than happy to quickly assure me that Rita's transfer could be taken care of—right away!

The timing was perfect—right before the semester break. Rita could begin at her new school the very day classes resumed.

Rita found out she knew more students than she thought. With a few exceptions, they welcomed her into the school. She was now in the middle of the tenth grade. We moved to a house even closer to the new high school, which provided the opportunity for more of her new classmates to come and visit. Her grades began to improve. Rita was happier than I'd seen her in a long time. She got a part-time job after school and gained some more independence and confidence. She no longer needed her New York friend's money to leave home.

Rita had a few challenges in her last two years of high school, but she had learned that change is not always bad. We'd become closer. She could talk to me about anything.

The experience she had at her first high school made her doubt the importance of a high school diploma. She wasn't sure she needed it. I asked her to think about her present clerk job. Would she want to do that, or that kind of job, all her life? She saw me, someone with a high school diploma and some college courses, struggling to find a good job. Rita decided to give school a chance, to really study her courses and do her homework.

On her graduation day, she told me she wanted to go back to her first high school, wearing her cap and gown, to let them know that she graduated. After previously making light of our city's small junior college, she attended and earned a two-year associate degree in business administration to go along with her high school diploma. She is now in her last year of a four-year college.

Rita and I rarely speak of the time when an assistant principal did not have a big enough belief in her future. Instead, we are spending most of our time exploring graduate schools for her.

BETH DUNCAN

IV
MORE THAN ENOUGH

*In our breathless attempts
we often miss the flowering that waits for afternoon.*

ANNE MORROW LINDBERGH

Her vocabulary was as bad as, like, whatever.
AUTHOR UNKNOWN

GOOD STOCK

"**Y**ou don't understand these things, but Tim's family comes from a different stock. His family ain't going to like you and it isn't gonna be because of something you do or how you look. Just stay home. Tim will be back in August."

"What are we, Ma? A herd of cows?" I ask, regretting this conversation and where it's going to lead.

"Yeah. They're Holsteins."

"And I'm just a low-quality milking cow, nothing else?"

"Not to me, but to them you are. Jerseys are good. Holsteins just think they're better. You're seventeen and you think Tim's gonna be the guy you marry, but it won't happen. You just graduated from high school. He's going to college. Tim ain't gonna stay in Michigan. His family's in New York."

"I'm not gonna stay in Michigan all my life."

"No, I'm sure you won't, but as nice as Tim is, you ain't gonna be marrying him."

I'm going to spend my one-week vacation in Schenectady and prove my mother wrong. She'll see that people with money and education view me as a person, not as a milking cow.

Tim's mother is a preschool teacher and his father's away on a business trip. I wear my nicest clothes and offer to help with all the chores, but I can tell his mother isn't impressed by me. She's always correcting her two youngest children's grammar, looking at me as if I need the same lessons.

My last night there I'm lying in my bed, and I hear his mother say, "If you keep dating that girl, we're not going to pay for your tuition. We're paying all that money to send you to a private college and you date a local girl who's not even going to go to college? What is wrong with you?"

"I'll talk to her about going to school, Mother."

"You're not going to be able to change her mind. Education doesn't mean anything to those kind of people."

The next day, I don't let Tim know I overheard their conversation. Maybe I'll enroll in a few college classes, but I'd rather work as a teacher's aide.

I return home and say nothing that would confirm my mother's fears. She's relieved I'm home and reminds me to send a gift and note to Tim's mother.

A week later, Tim writes me a brief letter: *"How could you write 'I want to thank all of youse'? What if the president invited us to his house and you sent that as your thank you note?"* Then he goes on to explain why "youse" is incorrect, and I wonder how I got through high school without learning that, then I remember the sneers I received when I said things wrong at his house.

My mother sees me crying and I show her the letter. "That fool ain't gonna be invited to the president's house. And if he is, let him write his own thank you notes. Those people are clods. Not one word from his mother saying thanks to you for those nice candlestick holders. If you ask me, you're too good for Tim. At least you got good manners and care about people. You dump him before he dumps you. His mother's gonna be pressuring him. Make life easy on yourself. Date someone who works at a factory."

Deep down, I know my mother's right. I will get dumped. Not

only does my mother want to prevent me from getting hurt, she's worried I'll cross that fence, that fence I fear I'll never cross, and join the Holsteins, thinking I'm too good for my family. But I want to prove her wrong. Show her that we are people, not cattle, and I'll never think I'm too good for my family, even if I do get a college education.

When I get dumped, not only will I be devastated; his mother will have won over my mother, another blue-ribbon victory for the Holsteins, another loss for the blue-collars. A loss my mother seems to already know. A loss that improved grammar wouldn't even be able to prevent.

Tim never knew that after he dumped me, I not only finished college, I got a job teaching English at a university. Finally, a victory for the milking cows.

DIANE PAYNE

IN THE SEA OF AVERAGE

"**C**ould try harder" and "Not working to potential" were the types of comments that usually showed up on my report cards throughout the years. It seemed the harder I worked at being on the coveted end of the bell curve, the more I bobbed right near center. Average in a sea of average, until late one afternoon in the fall of my sophomore year at high school. I wandered the campus searching for a friend to walk with me into town. When I finally found Lynette in the art lab, she was by herself kneading a wad of gray clay. "Let's get out of here," I said, elbows propped against her kneading board.

"I'm behind," she said. "I've got two weeks to come up with something symmetrical that doesn't explode when it's fired. I can't flunk art."

"Gimme some of that."

"You're not even supposed to be in here."

"Want me to leave?"

The clay felt cool and there was something about the give as I pressed into it that made everything else in my head fall away.

"Keep working it till there's no air." Lynette cut her ball of clay in half and held the halves open. "Totally smooth," she said. "That's what you want."

The hard slap of her clay hitting the wooden bat a minute later made me jump. She sat at the wheel, leg swinging and foot kicking the wheel base. The clay spun, lopsided at first, until she wet her hands and put them to it. The ball of clay rose to a cone then flattened to a squat cylinder. "Centering," she said.

I watched her for the rest of the afternoon, mesmerized by the spinning, the shape-shifting, but in the end her lopsided bowl wound up in the scrap bucket.

Two days later I kneaded spare balls of clay while she struggled with the one on the wheel. "I can't get this stupid thing centered."

"Let me try." At the wheel I dipped my hands into the water bucket.

"Kick," Lynette ordered. "The wheel's too slow."

I kicked, steadied both hands on the clay, and pressed. It rose easily into a cone. "Now press down, and keep your other hand against the cone." The cone flattened.

"Do it a couple more times, until the clay's spinning even."

She went to the table and took up the ball of clay I'd been kneading.

"Now what?" I asked once the clay was centered.

"Rest your hands against the outside of the cylinder and press your thumbs into the center. Pull out as you press down."

As a hole in the center of the clay opened under the pressure of my thumbs, a place in me opened to the clay. I'd never before had the feeling of complete absorption with the task at hand. Had never let go of the outcome or final product long enough to fully engage in the process.

Lynette glanced up from her kneading and rolled her eyes. "Beginner's luck," she said.

A small symmetrical bowl had taken shape under my hands. "Now what do I do?"

"Sponge the water out of the bottom. We'll put it on the shelf to dry and I've got something to turn in."

"No way!" I said.

"You're not even supposed to be here, remember?"

I decided it didn't matter, Lynette turning in my work. For the first time in my life, I didn't need the recognition that came with a final product. What mattered was getting my hands on some clay, and the stillness inside me as the clay spun and shape-shifted.

The art teacher started complimenting Lynette's progress. I knew because Lynette told me as she kneaded out my clay each afternoon. It was a sweet arrangement. She got the credit and I got to see what my hands would come up with next. Some pieces went in the scrap bucket, others on the shelf. It didn't matter where they wound up. Nothing mattered until the afternoon the art teacher walked in.

"Who're you?" She stood hands on hips, straight brown hair brushing her waist.

"I'm just fooling around," I said.

"This lab is for art students only," she said. "You need to leave."

I stopped the wheel and on my way to the door she held up a palm and said, "Just a minute." She glanced from the small symmetrical bowl on the wheel to Lynette kneading clay. "Get one of your pieces," she said to her.

Lynette took a leather-hard pot down from the shelf and handed it to the teacher, who then looked from the wheel to the piece in her hand, and finally at me. "You did this?"

I nodded, avoiding her eyes. My chest felt as if a twenty-five-pound bag of clay sat on it. I couldn't imagine life without the art room, the afternoons without slip under my nails, or my hands wet and soft and wrinkled.

"You," she pointed at Lynette, "do your own work. I don't care if it's lopsided. What I care about is that it's yours. And you," she had turned back to me. "Doing her work is cheating, so unless I'm going to turn both of you in, you need to sign up for an art class next term."

That was it? No trip to the principal's office? No lecture? Here was a teacher worth working for.

In ceramics during winter term I learned how to do what I'd been doing even better, and I spent every spare moment after school and on weekends at the wheel. Seeing my interest, she kept it piqued by teaching me the next step when I was ready, letting me move at my own pace. Spring term she met me during her time off and taught me how to fire the kiln and mix glazes. By the end of the year she had me firing everyone else's work, too.

On the verge of summer vacation we were unloading the kiln and closing down the art lab. I lifted out my final piece, a large white pot rimmed in cobalt blue, and handed it to her, still warm.

She turned it in her hands and said, "I've taught you everything I know."

The rounded bowl she held turned out slightly at the lip; my finger marks spiraled evenly up the sides. Part of me, yet separate, a product to be sold or given away, yet whatever it was in me that created that bowl was a gift, something way beyond average, and with me to stay.

BURKY ACHILLES

Life's ups and downs provide windows of opportunity
to determine your values and goals. Think of using all obstacles
as stepping stones to build the life you want.
MARSHA SINETAR

THROUGH MY EYES ONLY

I was little more than a ghost in elementary school;
everyone saw me, but no one knew I was there. My father
was in the military and we moved so often that friends
were something other people had—not me.

Many of the places we lived didn't have bases, so we rented
houses in the "civilian community." It was there I became invisible, in a crowd of children who'd attended school together most
of their lives.

It also didn't help that I was plain in a world where beauty was
prized above all. And, although I was a good student, I wasn't
scholarship material—just an ordinary kid with no visible signs
of talent. So I spent my early school days hanging around in
limbo, surrounded by people who neither knew me, nor cared.
But the anonymity of elementary school was nothing compared
to what turned out to be the torture of junior high.

We moved three times while I was in junior high. The
third time I attended a large school in a big city, with a well-developed social system. At the top of the social chain were the

cheerleaders—goddesses in saddle shoes and swingy skirts. They wore sweaters with the school letter on them and had megaphones with their names printed on them. They went steady with the athletes and took all the honors—from starring in school plays to homecoming court.

For the most part, the rest of us just didn't count. Oh, there were a couple of non-cheerleaders who were allowed into the sacred circle—a girl who was funny, the head of the drill team, and a few others. But it was the cheerleading squad that held all the other girls' attention.

How I longed to be one! I remember watching them and wondering how it felt to be beautiful and the center of attention. In my teenage world, there was nothing, absolutely nothing, more wonderful than being a cheerleader.

I watched them during the pep rallies as they led cheers. I knew everything about them—their names, who they dated, and who their friends were. Only one of them ever spoke to me: a sweet girl named Sarah who was more down to earth than the others. But I spent most of that year in obscurity. Even the faculty played the popularity game. The "in" kids were treated differently than the rest of us and everybody knew it.

When the school play was cast, I tried out and won a small part as the villain. There was a boy in the cast named Jon and I had a hopeless crush on him. But I was colorless and he never even spoke to me.

But my agony did have a stopping point. Dad was transferred to a duty station where we stayed for only a few weeks, then we were sent overseas. I ended up in a military dependents' high school in Japan.

My first day of school there was the best day I'd had in my life up to that point. The kids there knew what it was like to be new and friendless and they took my hand and introduced me around. Within a few weeks, I felt as though I'd lived there forever.

Not only did I make friends, I also got involved in school. I ran for and won a spot on student council. I tried out for and nailed a great role in the school play, and I didn't have to play a villain.

I had a boyfriend and a best friend and knew everyone, and when a new kid came in, I made sure I was one of the first to say hello and offer a hand in friendship.

We stayed there until I graduated and then I went back to the United States for college—back to the place where I attended junior high in obscurity. Back to where Jon lived.

It turned out that Jon was in a fraternity with a guy I knew and he set us up on a date. I couldn't believe it. My crush, the boy I couldn't even speak to, was taking me out.

I must have spent three hours preparing for that date and when I floated downstairs, I was a different girl than the one who played the villain in the junior high play. I looked great and felt like a million dollars. I was confident and full of myself when I walked into the dorm lobby to see him for the first time in several years.

But when he stood up, I didn't recognize him. *Surely,* I thought, *the guy I had the crush on was taller. And I know he was much more handsome.* The boy standing in front of me was unremarkable . . . and ordinary.

Jon brought me up to date on the cheerleaders I worshipped. For the most part they'd married straight out of high school or drifted into unremarkable careers. He was in college, but wasn't sure where he was going.

I told him about traveling around the world, living in a foreign culture, having friends who also lived around the globe. We talked of the travails of junior high and the teachers. By the end of the evening he was asking if he could call me again.

And I said, "No. You're a nice guy, but not my type. Nor am I yours."

Years later, I heard the junior high had some kind of reunion. I just laughed. By that time I was working for an ABC affiliate as an on-camera news reporter. I'd been to the Middle East and Europe, met senators, generals, and diplomats.

I was no longer ordinary, but then, I never really was. I just saw myself through the eyes of other people—people who dismissed me without knowing me. Now I know that the only opinion of myself that really counts is mine. And today that's the only person I try to please.

CAROLE MOORE

MOLLY'S PORTRAIT

"**C**an I get my portrait done?" asked my thirteen-year-old daughter, Molly, tapping my arm. "Please, Mom?"
"Here?" I asked. Portrait artists crowded the dark perimeter of the Montmartre Place du Tertre, waiters with trays full of drinks cursed the hordes, tacky souvenir vendors barked and beckoned. The fourteenth-century square, once home to real artists and Bohemians, was now all noise and neon.

But there was something in Molly's voice. This wasn't your everyday pleading for an Arc de Triomphe pencil sharpener or a Marie Antoinette-in-a-silver-guillotine charm. It reminded me of a year earlier when Molly resolved—with courage and great determination—to attend her first boy-girl party. Not a time for the maternal knee-jerk no.

I looked at my friend Arlene who rolled her eyes; her eleven-year-old Emma was making a similar request, somewhat less compelling. "Let's just go look," I finally said to Molly as Emma and Arlene disappeared into the crowd. "But I'm not making any promises."

Our excursion had begun impulsively on a hot summer night in Paris with seven cheerful, overfed people jammed into a borrowed station wagon with a moon roof. It was too early to call it quits, and majority ruled: Montmartre at midnight it would be.

When we reached the top of the hill, husbands and son set off to find tall glasses of *citron pressé* in a faux Bohemian sidewalk café, while we surveyed the artistic talent.

Business was brisk; almost every artist, cigarette dangling, charcoal or pastel in hand, squinted into the face of some giggling, self-conscious foreigner. Hungry caricaturists drew grotesque cartoons that insulted their subjects. Other artists concentrated on making innocent prepubescent girls—like ours—look like brainless, big-eyed nymphs.

"You like these?" I asked Molly.

"They look pretty, Mom."

"You think?" My reluctance to get behind this idea wavered, however, when we came upon an older man with a weathered face and shaggy gray hair, smoking quietly on a lawn chair as he watched the crowds stroll by. He looked tired and sad and maybe a little disappointed in himself. Beside him, in pastels, was a drawing that looked *exactly like him.* Every wrinkle, his rumpled shirt, his uncombed hair. This old guy had soul.

"What about *him?*" I whispered to Molly.

She hesitated.

"This is the one," I said. "I'll say yes to this one."

I bent forward to ask how much. He murmured something reasonable as he slowly rose to his feet. I nodded. He looked at Molly for a long moment, unsmiling, then beckoned for her to sit on the high stool in front of his easel. When I took a hairbrush out of my purse to redo Molly's ponytail, he tapped my shoulder and shook his head no. *Just the way she is,* he seemed to say.

Molly began picking her cuticles. I positioned myself behind the artist, pantomimed nail picking so she'd stop, and smiled encouragingly.

He lit a fresh cigarette. Then he assembled his pastels, pulled out a sheet of gray paper, and turned on a small light to illuminate Molly's face. A few people stopped in the dark to watch.

She looked small and brave sitting there on the stool, plastic butterflies bouncing on springs in her hair.

She doesn't smile, exactly; she even looks somewhat defiant. Also, vulnerable and a little sad. Complex. He'll never capture this.

He works slowly, hypnotically. For a long time, nothing appears to be happening—just lonely lines and random strokes. But then an image begins to materialize from the gray paper like a defrosting windshield.

My husband, Dan, leaves his lemonade and comes to stand behind me. When I turn to him I notice a small crowd has formed, maybe ten people all watching in silence. Molly seems unaware of them. Occasionally someone whispers, but otherwise I hear nothing but the sound of my own heartbeat.

Her face continues to emerge, lifelike, unsettling.

Suddenly I was scared. This wasn't going to be what Molly had in mind. I'd made a terrible mistake. I watched until I could no longer bear it, and then I left Dan to do the reassuring while I went in search of Arlene and Emma.

I jostled my way through the crowds and finally saw Emma sitting in a tall director's chair, her thick brown hair flowing down her shoulders, her big blue-green eyes smiling optimistically. Arlene looked disgusted and I soon saw why: The young artist was amusing himself by making Emma look like Monica Lewinsky.

When I returned, Molly raised her eyebrows at me, wanting to know how her portrait was coming. I moved around to see.

There on the gray paper her eyes have emerged, deep and dark, searching and sad. Lonely. There is the discoloration, the hint of swelling under her right brow, the noticeable asymmetry of her face, the blue translucence of her skin. There are the tired tendrils of blonde hair escaped from her ponytail, the bangs I accidentally cut too short, the bouncy butterflies.

I look at her on the stool, at her in the portrait, at the artist concentrating—fully immersed in the effort to capture exactly what he perceives. I watch him, the way he studies her face, the way his eyes move back and forth between her face and his easel, back and forth, holding delicately between thumb and forefinger a bit of yellow crayon. He whispers into the portrait with his fingers a hint of yellow, a tiny bit of white, an intimation of green, and blends gently with his thumb. Ashes fall from the cigarette hanging from his mouth, unnoticed.

Another man, an older man with paint under his big finger-nails, sets a beer down next to our artist. He nods briefly in thanks, continuing to gaze steadily at Molly. The friend stays to watch.

The crowd behind us continues to grow.

I watch them, wondering how much of Molly's story these strangers can guess. Certainly not the months in intensive care, or the neurological damage, or the epilepsy. Do they notice her hear-ing aids? Do they mistake her small stature for that of a much younger child? Do they suspect the inoperable tumor behind her right eye?

She sits tall and very still. She wants what other girls have: to be made beautiful, to be seen as beautiful. She looks directly into his eyes, without artifice or fear. She is determined, almost fierce, and in all that animates her, she is lovely. She is luminous and alive.

My throat constricts, my cheeks are wet. I find I'm crying.

A woman in the crowd steps toward me and pats my shoulder tenderly. When I turn toward her, she is smiling. Her eyelashes are wet. Her face looks rapturous, like God's face. *"Très jolie,"* she says with a German accent. Lovely.

"Oui," I say. *"Merci."*

Minutes pass, maybe an hour, or more. The crowd has swollen into a small congregation.

Finally, the artist stands back, squints, adds a blue background shadow and small brown tick marks to help with framing. He writes quickly in charcoal *Victor Romanoff. Paris 1999. Montmartre* and then he wipes his hands on his pants.

Molly hopped off the stool and came around to see. I stood be-hind her, holding her shoulders.

"Oh," she said quietly.

"What do you think?"

"I . . . *that* doesn't look like me." Her face, first so hopeful, sagged with disappointment. "Does it?"

I turned quickly to Victor Romanoff and smiled, taking out

my wallet, handing him a wad of bills. He continued to watch her dispassionately.

"*Merci beaucoup,*" I said as he rolled the portrait in a sheet of waxed paper and handed it to Molly, bowing slightly. Molly provided a perfunctory nod and crept away to find Emma.

Victor Romanoff lit a fresh cigarette and took a long drink of beer.

"Monsieur Romanoff," I began, looking into his deep-set eyes, "I really appreciate the way you—"

"Sorry," he said with a thick Russian accent, shaking his head. "I no speak English."

"Oh," I nodded. But then his friend, the man who brought the beer, stepped closer, saying something in Russian. Victor nodded and for the first time, he smiled.

"Do *you* speak English?" I asked the friend.

"Yes."

"Could you tell Mr. Romanoff . . . that I . . . that he really captured something in my daughter? And that it hurts to see it but that I . . ."

The friend began translating into Russian. Victor Romanoff looked at his feet and listened, nodding.

When the friend paused and turned to me, I continued, ". . . it hurts to see what you saw, but also it is . . . deeply—"

Again the friend translated until Victor Romanoff interrupted. He looked directly into my eyes and said something in Russian.

"He say, 'Only I paint what I see. What I see in your girl many things. She is beauty. As God make her.' "

"Yes," I said, tears flowing. "She is beautiful."

"Yes. She is beautiful," Victor Romanoff repeated in English. And then he began to set up for his next portrait.

Lesley Quinn

The only people with whom you should try to get even
are those who have helped you.
MAY MALOO

HOMECOMING HERO

*I*t was two weeks before the Homecoming Dance my senior year in high school, and I was planning to attend the
event with my boyfriend. Mark and I had been dating for almost a full year at this point and while we weren't the most popular couple, I felt happy that I had found someone smart and funny
who really cared about me. Mark was always thoughtful; calling
me a couple times a week just to say hello and taking me out to
the movies, but this was a big deal.

I had been planning the details for months with my best friend
Debby. We had decided on everything from our dresses—mine
was burgundy velvet with a slit my mother didn't approve of,
and hers was navy blue satin without straps that her father didn't
approve of—to an itinerary for the big day—lunch at my house,
then manicures, then her house to get ready.

There was, however, one thing we hadn't planned on: Mark
calling me and breaking up with me. He told me on the phone
that he had met a pretty freshman, Kimberly, who worked with
him on the school newspaper. He told me that he just didn't want
to go out anymore and that he was sorry but he wanted to take
Kimberly to the dance. I was crushed. Devastated actually, but the

smart part of my heart knew that I didn't want to be with someone who didn't want to be with me. I still wanted to go to the Homecoming Dance, yet all of my male friends were already going.

I cried and cried and told my mother that I was never leaving my bedroom. She tried to lure me out with Girl Scout Samoas. My mother felt terrible and so did Debby, who made me a card that read *Cinderella went stag*. But I knew that I had to produce a date if I wanted to hold my head up at the dance.

I was sitting in my room feeling sorry for myself when the doorbell rang. I really didn't want to answer it but since I was the only one home, I didn't have a choice. There in the doorway, wearing a Gap sweatshirt and jeans, was my next door neighbor, Mike. He had tortured me like an older brother since I was a small child. Mike and I used to play G.I. Joe in his backyard. Though he'd never admit it to his soccer buddies in college, he used to sometimes let me use G.I. Joe for a military wedding with my Barbie dolls. He used to call me "pygmy" because I went through a phase where I had long legs and arms and a potbelly and looked like one we saw in *National Geographic*. Mike had blue eyes and brown hair and was a biology major and freshman at Bucknell University.

He paused and then began, "Hey, pygmy, my mom told me that you had a little high school boyfriend who didn't have the sense to hold on to a good thing when he had it. I was thinking. I'll be home till the middle of January, so if you still need a date, I guess that I could find the time." He smiled and added, "I'd be honored to take you."

"Yes!" I shouted and gave him a big hug. Mike and I had grown apart as we got older but I hadn't even considered that he would be home. Now, not only did I have a date, I had a hot college guy to take me.

Mike was the cutest guy at the dance. He looked stunning in his suit and I even caught Kimberly giving him a glance. Mike gave me a corsage with burgundy roses and danced with me all night. He was my Homecoming Hero, G.I. Joe style, arriving to rescue me in the nick of time. We had such a wonderful night he's already agreed to escort me to the Senior Prom in June.

SUSAN LAMAIRE

THE PRETTY PEOPLE

"**W**hat on earth do you see in him?" I challenged my older sister. "He's not good looking at all!"

Both of us could be called lovely Scottish lasses, with standards to uphold when it came to boyfriends.

"Looks aren't everything," Linda said in typical older-sister-who-knows-more-than-you fashion. "He's a great guy."

I decided she might be older, but not wiser. My own viewpoint was much more practical. "That might be so, but Eric's a great guy *and* he's good looking."

I had only been out with Eric a couple of times when I uttered those wise words to my sister, and I knew they must be true. But that same week, Eric called to cancel our date. "Sorry, but the guys are all going to see the Red Sox game, and we're making a weekend of it." No other explanation. He was putting me second to baseball. What a cheek!

My eyes soon landed on Wayne, though. I asked my friends if they thought he was cute and they said he was. *Mission accomplished,* I thought, quite satisfied. Still, my sister cautioned me, "Watch out for Wayne. He's a bit of a Romeo."

Much to my chagrin, I had to admit she was right about Wayne. Halfway through our first date, his hands were all over me. That made two cheeky lads, but I knew the next fellow would be better. So when a new family moved onto the street and my sister mentioned they had an eighteen-year-old son, I immediately asked, "Is he good looking?" Linda shot back an annoyed look, but I met it with steadfast defiance. Which wasn't worth much because I found out this new neighbor, Lee, wasn't good looking. Not to my standards. He was kind of studious instead, so when he asked me out, I quickly refused.

Linda called me an idiot, which didn't surprise me. But it did surprise me when my best pal, Angie, started going out with him. "Why, for heaven's sake?" I asked.

Angie shrugged my comment off, which surprised me even more. "Because Lee's great fun. I really enjoy being with him."

I had to shake my head as we went to class. I'd heard those platitudes before, and they bored me. As we settled into our seats, our assignment was to say whom we admired, who would be our role models? One or two people said ancients, like Leonardo da Vinci. Someone else said Walt Disney. I said "Elle Macpherson or Cindy Crawford."

My teacher sighed. "Always the pretty people, Joyce. One day you will learn how shallow a choice that is."

Since my teacher was plain and frumpy, I gave that the credibility it deserved.

Angie and I were still quite close, even with our differences in date material. But when the tele rang and Mum said, "Oh no! Oh how awful, I'll tell Joyce—" I had no idea it would be about my best friend. As I glanced at her, time seemed to stop its motion, and I still remember each step as she walked across the living room. I knew something terrible must have happened. "Angie has been in a car crash. She's pretty badly hurt."

"Oh no, not Angie," I heard myself say as tears flooded my eyes. Then thinking twice, I knew she must've been on a date. "What about Lee?"

Mum shook her head. "Lee didn't survive."

In the quiet that fell like a shroud, I felt Angie's grief surround me. She had really fallen for Lee, and I knew she would be devastated. For so many reasons, she would need me now.

When Mum and I walked up to Angie's bed, I almost fainted. Her lovely face was barely recognizable. It wasn't just swollen eyes and bruising. Her face had been split open and she was covered in bandages and stitches, her jaw was wired. Maybe mercifully, Angie was too drugged to know I was there.

Two days later Mum frowned at me. "Why on earth haven't you been round to see Angie?"

I bit my lip. Not willing to confess I couldn't bear to see her all horrible and disfigured, I used a "not feeling well" excuse. I used it as long as I could, until finally one day I went to my part-time job at the pet store and promised to visit Angie afterward.

Work should keep my mind busy, and it did. So when a family of four came in, I barely glanced up. As they looked over the kittens, the mother said to the younger boy, "Well, this is going to be your kitten. They all look much the same, mind you."

His older brother suddenly spotted one. "Oh, except that one. Is that out of the same litter?"

"Yes," I said. "Odd really. All the others are lovely marked cats, but she has those odd-shaped black bits over one eye and her mouth."

Immediately the younger boy said, "I'll have her, the one with the black bits!"

I frowned at him, as the others were really lovely cats. "Are you sure? You see, she won't get any prettier as she gets older."

The boy raised his face to look at me. "I'm blind. As long as she loves me, I'll see her as beautiful."

I stared at him in silence as his brother picked up the kitten he wanted and gave it to him. Outside afterward, I saw the little boy put the kitten up to his face. She was rubbing up against him and purring. He was right, he had found something beautiful.

As soon as they left, I went straight to the hospital.

"Joyce? Oh Joyce, I am so glad to see you. I feel so alone," Angie barely got the words out as she started to cry. And even after I offered my help, her grief was not contained. "I'll have such scars though," she said as more tears ran down her cheeks.

"They can do great things, probably very little will show," I said at first, then added, "Angie, it won't matter. You are such a great person, no one on earth will care that you have a few odd marks on your face."

"You'll care. I won't ever be one of your pretty people again!"

Stunned at first by the mirror of my self, my own tears sprang into my eyes.

"Thank goodness for that. I've been blind, Angie!" I licked one of my tears off my mouth as I painted a new picture for my good friend.

"You and I can do this together. And you can be my real role model, Angie, someone who came through an awful ordeal with flying colors. And I'll be here, where I am now, at your side."

In that moment, time graciously slowed down again. And as Angie's hand touched mine, I felt her scoop up the tiny odd-marked kitty—of me. And for maybe the first time in my life, in the most remarkable of ways, I felt truly beautiful inside.

JOYCE STARK

HALFTIME HIGHLIGHTS

Isighed as I walked toward study hall. Only a month until eighth-grade graduation, four months until I started high school, and I was miserable. I had been painfully shy my whole life. In class, I was too scared to raise my hand. Sometimes I would finish first when we took tests, but I'd wait until a bunch of other kids were turning their papers in to the teacher so I could go up in a group. When I walked to and from school, I slouched and hung my head—not wanting to take up too much space in the world.

In fact, I quit the junior high choral group because I was too scared to perform. I wouldn't speak up in public even if someone offered me my weight in gold. I hated myself for being so shy. I didn't want to suffer this way through high school, and I decided to do something about it.

But what? I stopped by the bulletin board to see what was for lunch and a flyer caught my eye. The high school band camp was going to be starting in a few weeks. They performed at halftime during football season; surely no one in band could be shy. I didn't play a musical instrument, though. Then I read the bottom of the flyer—they were looking for girls to join the flag squad! It said that the squad marched in formation and twirled big flags while the band played. Well, I could do that. Maybe this would be a good way to make myself get over being so shy.

After school I went to the band director's office and stammered, "Um, I'd like to try out for the flag squad."

The band director didn't say much; he just handed me a form

for my mom to fill out and a brochure on when band camp started.

Well, I thought, it looks like I'm on my way.

Camp was held at the high school a few weeks later. I felt a little intimidated by all the older girls in the squad even though they were really nice. I was afraid I'd be the worst person there, but another girl kept forgetting which foot was left and which one was right. Finally the band director got so mad, he put an "L" on her left shoe and an "R" on the right one.

She's much worse than I am, I thought. *At least I know my feet!*

We practiced during the day and at night, and I'd practice in my backyard. At first, the flag was really hard to handle because the pole was about six feet long, and when I twirled and marched, I wobbled all over the place. It took a little while for my arms to get stronger but as they did, I got better. I liked the snapping sound the flag made as it went around. I didn't wobble as much when I marched. And I always knew my left from my right.

When high school started in the fall, it didn't seem as scary as I thought it would. Sure, there were lots of students I didn't know, but in every class I'd recognize someone from band camp, someone who knew me and would say Hi. They introduced me to their friends and I met more and more people. Suddenly, raising my hand in class didn't seem so frightening. Even better, I had people to sit with at lunch.

One test remained though. I still had to perform with the flag squad during halftime of the football games. There would be a few hundred people in the stands. I was nervous, but I had to be there; I couldn't let my friends down. I practiced even more, studying the index card that had my marching and twirling directions until I could almost do it in my sleep.

Finally the night of the first home game arrived. I got to wear my uniform for the first time—a heavy maroon polyester skirt, a maroon and white polyester shirt, white boots, and a maroon cowboy-type hat. It might sound awful, but I was proud to wear it.

The band sat in the stands for most of the first half and cheered on the football team. I enjoyed sitting with the squad and yelling. Before I knew it, it was time to get ready. We lined up in the end zone with only a few minutes left in the first half. I was scared. What if I messed up? Everyone would see me. Would they laugh?

Once we marched onto the field, I didn't have time to be scared. We went through all the routines and I didn't make one mistake! I twirled my flag and marched and didn't wobble once. I stayed in perfect formation through the whole performance. At the end of halftime, the crowd cheered. They were cheering for the whole band, but it felt like it was all for me.

I did it! I went in front of people and nothing bad happened. No one laughed and I didn't trip. I felt a lot more confident after that, like I could do anything I wanted.

By the time I graduated, I had acted in school plays, started a small newspaper, and never hesitated to speak up in class. I knew that if I tried hard enough, I could overcome any fear. Since graduation, I've worked as a disc jockey, read my poetry in public, and given several speeches. I can trace all these successes back to one decision I made before high school. To take a step into the unknown—away from being shy and toward a goal—all with the twirl of a flag.

SHARON WREN

V

YOUNG WISDOM
ROCKS

Peace and joy are what is left
when we stop doing everything else.

CHERI HUBER

THE ELEMENT OF TRUTH

I
had a boyfriend in high school who was creative, hu-
morous, smart, and independent. I loved his company but I
was never totally comfortable with him. He was as creative
with the truth as he was with everything else.

We were in the same chemistry class. Chemistry was hard for
me. I couldn't master the subject, even though I studied. I worked
hard to get the mediocre grades that I had. Once or twice I asked
my boyfriend to tutor me, but he always made an excuse. He
didn't think it was important.

"Why bother?" he said. "You'll never use it."

I studied anyway. When a test came up, I studied even more.

On the day of the midterm, I was a wreck. I looked around for
my boyfriend but he wasn't in class yet. The teacher handed out
the test papers and still his seat was empty. He came in late with
his hand wrapped in a big white bandage. He told the teacher he
had a bad sprain. It might even be a hairline fracture, I heard him
say. He couldn't write. Our teacher excused him from the test. He
winked at me as he left the room. Now I was worried about him,
as well as passing the midterm.

"How is your hand?" I asked when I saw him in the lunchroom
three periods later.

He laughed and held it up. There was no bandage, and as he
moved his hand around I could see that there was no injury, either.
He laughed at the confusion on my face.

"I made it up," he said. "I didn't feel like studying so I invented
a sore hand. Did you think I really hurt myself?"

"Of course I did," I told him. "Why wouldn't I?"

"Boy, are you gullible," he said. "Look, I didn't really lie. I couldn't write because I didn't know the answers. I'll take the test another time when I'm ready. No one was hurt. Gotta go."

I watched him take his tray back and head for the door. A group of his friends joined him. He must have been telling them about what he did because they were hooting. When they turned to look at me and laughed even harder, I knew he was telling them about how I had believed him.

I sat at the lunch table until the bell rang, thinking. To him, he wasn't lying. To me, he wasn't telling the truth. He was happy. I was struggling.

My chemistry test came back a week later with a barely passing grade. I looked at the formulas I had written—some correct, some wrong—and thought that my boyfriend was right. I probably would never have use for anything I was learning in the chemistry book. But I had learned something valuable from that chemistry class. There is no formula for integrity, yet it's an essential element in a relationship and in life. If he faked the things he thought were unimportant, what would he do when something big came up?

I never found out if my boyfriend took a make-up test because I stopped seeing him. Our chemistry was no longer there.

FERIDA WOLFF

BRAINS, BOOKS, AND BOYS

Walking back home, backpack filled with books, I see Grandpa sitting on his porch swing, and I cross the street to join him.

"Whattya have in that heavy bag?" he asks.

"Books."

"Don't be wasting your hard-earned money on books!"

"I didn't buy them, Grandpa. I was at the library," I say, quietly regretting that I didn't own them.

"You're never gonna get a husband if you keep reading all those books. If you smile nice at the restaurant, a nice boy will ask you on a date. But, if he finds out about those books, he won't date you. You get too smart, and the boys lose interest. Just smile at them. Don't say too much."

"Oh, Grandpa! It's not like that anymore. Only families go to the restaurant, and old people. Boys don't hang out at Veurink's Kitchen. And it doesn't matter how much I smile at those customers, they don't tip anyway."

"Oh, they pay enough to eat there. They shouldn't have to tip."

"Want to play Aggravation?" I say. Grandpa made the game board himself, and I think it's just the game we need right now.

We go inside his apartment and he hauls out the heavy board. Grandma is cleaning houses today. Even though neither of them reads, Grandma would have rolled her eyes so Grandpa couldn't have seen her if she had heard Grandpa make that comment about books and boys. The only book in their home is the Bible, and it's written in Dutch.

We say nothing while we play the game. Grandpa prefers it to be quiet, but he doesn't really like to be alone. Every morning after he sees that we've walked past his house on the way to school, he heads over to have coffee with Mom in the kitchen. I wonder what they could possibly talk about, since neither seems to be great conversationalists. I do know they enjoy speaking in Dutch and figure they probably cut out coupons, and Grandpa is probably checking on Mom to make sure she's okay and we have food in our cupboards.

"I remember when you were born," Grandpa says. In many ways, I think I'm Grandpa's favorite grandkid because he brought Mom to the hospital when I was born. "Your ma called me and said to hurry. We never used hospitals. The women had their babies at home. None of this fancy hospital stuff."

"If I ever have a baby, I think I'll do it at home with a midwife," I tell Grandpa.

"Nah, you go to the hospital. You won't get a husband if you keep reading those books."

"What am I going to do in college if I don't read books?"

"You ain't going to college. Girls don't need all that fancy schooling. You go to college after you've been in the military and the GI Bill pays for it. Your dad can get you a good job at the factory. That's where you'll meet a good husband."

I start conjuring up images of the men I'll meet who are like my dad, and this makes me more determined to never work at GM.

"I don't want to work at a factory or waitress all my life. I want to be a teacher or social worker. I need to go to college."

"Who's going to pay for all that?"

"I will."

"Things ain't the same no more," Grandpa says, getting that sad look that comes too quickly. "I win," he says, sounding like Eeyore from the Pooh books, which makes me laugh, but he doesn't know why. Grandpa starts picking up the game, his way of saying it's time to go.

Walking past the five houses between our homes, I wave and shout greetings to all the neighbors sitting on their steps. Feeling the books pound against my back, I wonder how I'll ever make it into college. Even if I don't get to go, I'll still keep reading, and I'll never have a boyfriend who doesn't appreciate books. Looking at all the houses on our block, I realize how few contain a bookshelf, how few people have even graduated from high school; but somehow I know I'll live in a house with bookshelves. And I'll have boyfriends who read books with me, and I'll still be playing Aggravation with Grandpa.

DIANE PAYNE

To gain that which is worth having
it may be necessary to lose everything.
BERNADETTE DEVLIN

WITHOUT HIM

"I don't want to do this anymore," I said in a voice not much louder than a whisper.

"Do what?" he asked.

"This—us," I proclaimed a little louder.

"What do you mean, you don't want to do this?" he snapped.

Seeing his anger start to boil, I said timidly, "Please just let me be by myself."

His eyes blazed as he grabbed me by my throat, spewing all kinds of profanities at me. "You're being stupid as usual, I'm the best thing that ever happened to you, you little dumb tramp. Without me, you're nothing." With that, he shoved me to the floor and stalked out of the room. I just lay there in a heap, sobbing, wondering if there was any way out of this.

Larry and I had grown up in the same neighborhood, but didn't start to have feelings for each other until we were fifteen. In high school we were hooked up by a mutual friend. Our relationship grew serious quickly, but almost grounded to a halt after my mother met him for the first time.

"I don't like that boy," she told me. "He's sneaky and he seems possessive."

Set to make her like him, he poured on the charm and her feelings swiftly turned to praise.

"He's good for you. He treats you right and he's a respectful young man," Mom said.

He fooled her like he fooled everybody, including me.

At first, he treated me like I was his princess. Anything I wanted or needed, he bought. He told me how much he loved me every day, and he smothered me with hugs and kisses. We motivated each other and even got after-school jobs at the same grocery store so we'd have money to do things together.

He loved to read whatever I wrote and said I was really talented. Writing has been my biggest aspiration in life and, being with him, his kindness and sensitivity inspired me to pour my feelings onto paper, creating beautiful poems and love letters for him. Even though my plate was full with school, my part-time job, and writing, I still made time for him. I was in love. I was his; no one could come between us. No one could hurt me.

Except him.

The first time he hit me, I just crumpled to the floor, my heart crushed. How could someone who loves me treat me this way? How could he actually take his fist and punch me? I thought he said he'd never hurt me. I thought I was his princess.

Did I leave him? No. I couldn't. When he "broke down" and said he was sorry, my heart wanted so badly to believe him because, without him, what would I do? Where would I be? Without him, who would I be?

The abuse continued throughout our three-year relationship. The poetry and letters that he used to devour so eagerly, he now tossed back at me when I asked him to read them. I was desperately seeking his approval. Because of his slashing critiques and insults, I began to just write, not bothering to ask for his opinion, because all he'd do was shatter my confidence even more.

Regardless of the punishment, the endless crying, slaps to the face, and punches and kicks, I stayed. Each time he apologized, and I forgave him. What else could I do? What he told me was that no one would treat me better than he did, it was my fault, my big mouth was what made him hit me. After losing all of my self-esteem, I believed every insulting word.

Things got so bad that I tried to distance myself from him by getting a job at a different grocery store. Even though that caused a vicious fight, I stood my ground and did it anyway.

At my new job, I met a guy and we began to like each other. However, because of Larry, I wouldn't start anything with him. Larry would constantly show up at my job unannounced to "check up on me" and, plenty of times, he caught me talking to that one particular guy. He couldn't wait to get me outside of the store to call me all kinds of degrading names.

I continued to talk to the guy at work anyway because he was so different from my boyfriend, and I really liked that. When I was with him, I was able to forget that my life was in shambles. It got to the point where he was all I could think about, day and night. Of course I had to get it on paper. I sat and wrote what flowed to my mind and ended up with a poem I called "Thoughts on You."

Just as I finished, Larry came and asked me what I was doing. I told him I was writing a poem. In a mocking tone, he said, "I guess you want me to read it, huh?" I told him I really didn't care because all he'd do was belittle it anyway. He snatched the poem from me and slowly began to read. I could see the fury building in his eyes after just the first two lines. Before even finishing, he balled the paper up and threw it at me. He snatched me out of the chair by my shirt and said, "Who is this bull crap about, is it about that boy I always catch you flirting with at work?"

That was when I told him I didn't want to be with him anymore. That was also when he choked me, "trying to strangle some sense into me." As I lay on the floor sobbing, the only way I could see getting away was if I left—left this world permanently, left all the pain and hurt behind me—for good.

How would he feel? Would he cry for me, like I'd cried so

many times before because of him? Would he even care if I killed myself?

Looking in the mirror, the pills in my hand, I stood trembling, tears streaming down my face. I didn't want to die; I didn't want to leave this world. I just wanted the pain to go away. But I thought I had no other choice; like he'd told me more times than I could count, I was nothing without him.

As I put the first tiny pill to my lip, it hit me. Without him, I'm still *me*. Without him, I'm still the beautiful girl who looks in the mirror and marvels at how pretty she is. Without him, I'm still the phenomenal young woman who knows what she wants in life and how to get it. Without him, I'm still lovable and able to love. Without him, I'm able to move on with my life and find someone who'll make me happy and treat me like a queen.

But most of all, without him, I'm alive.

TAMEKIA REECE

We don't know who we are until we see what we can do.
MARTHA GRIMES

THE STRENGTH TO CHANGE

That it has taken me more than twenty-one years to discover who I am lies in what I could do, and not in what I couldn't. In what I was, and not what I wasn't. Until I was eighteen, I thought my life would always be destined for unhappiness. I was obese, I was overweight, and I wasn't myself. At 258 pounds, I could play the denial game better than anyone I knew. It didn't bother me. I hadn't shopped in a section with "normal" sizes since I was small. As a kid I knew "pretty plus" sizes very well. I still think to myself *"Pretty Plus"* . . . *pretty, plus what? Plus a little cushion? Pretty plus fat?* I seemed to feel more "plus" than pretty whenever I dragged my feet into that pinker section of the store.

To feel better I interpreted that childhood label to mean that not only was I pretty like small girls, I was made of much, much more. I was tougher than the petite pixies whose lives seemed so simple. Because I was big I had to be funnier, smarter, and more outgoing to show that my fat did not slow me down. I hoped the laughter I brought my friends would mute the rolls that fell over my jeans. It worked in my mind for years.

It was two years ago, during my second season working as a Sea World photographer, that I began to feel the heft of my weight.

The sixty-plus hours a week became a torture for me as I squirmed under the fiery press of the Texas sun. I watched the thinner girls complain about their makeup melting while boys would fight to be photographed by them. I realized how much sweatier I seemed to be than the crew I worked with. My lungs would struggle up the stadium stairs we had to climb after every animal photo shoot. I loved taking pictures, but hated being in them. And, at the same time, it was lonely never being in a photo. I knew my life could not get any worse, and it was time for a change.

I had prayed for years to wake up thin, until I realized that I must make my own miracle. I quit the job that ate up my time and joined a local gym. From then on, I gained strength and a glimpse of reality I had never experienced before. I had always put off working out because I knew it would take a year or more to lose the amount of weight I wanted to. I realized during that summer that time would go by whether I was doing something good for myself or not. The year would pass by and I could either be working on losing weight or I could waste the time and dream of a goal that just wouldn't happen by itself.

I began by meeting with a trainer and dedicating five days a week to working out. I pushed myself hard to show the members that although I was big, I was determined. I would struggle to pedal faster than the people beside me in cycling classes. I challenged myself to keep up with the thinner friends I made at the gym. Those friends soon became my fans as my efforts shone through the weight I lost.

To help make this a lifestyle change, I watched what I ate with a strictness I had never thought possible for myself. Gone were extra helpings and empty calories such as sodas and sweets. As I ate, I thought, *How does this piece of food help my body?* The dream of a thin me became more appetizing than any piece of food could ever be.

With the support of family and friends, I lost my insecurity and gained the confidence I had wanted for so long in my life. I lost more than a hundred pounds that year, and I have kept it off since then.

My life is different in many ways, and I am much happier now that I can be comfortable in my own skin. Through my experiences as fat and now as thinner, I have learned many things about life. I feel that I have more than one set of eyes through which to see the world. From these two different lives, I have learned compassion, the power of persistence and dedication, and above all, I have gained a deeper understanding of the power of faith. Without the certainty God instilled in me that my weight loss was possible, I would have never been so brave as to really try. I believe that because this challenge was presented to me, my character was able to gain an inner beauty that could never be measured on a scale.

MELISSA SANDY VELA

Any parent—or otherwise clueless adult—
knows the quickest solution to computer problems:
Call a teenager.
KRISTI TURNQUIST

CYBER CHITCHAT

I'm glad we teach spelling in our schools. That way,
our children can busy themselves unlearning it when they
log on to the Internet.

One day last week, I stood and watched my thirteen-year-old
"chat" with some friends via e-mail. I thought I'd take the opportunity to monitor the electronic conversation being passed between these preteens—who long ago decided the telephone
wasn't good enough for them.

Looking over her shoulder, I very quickly found that I needed a
translator to decipher what was being said. Squinting down at the
monitor, I asked my daughter, "What kind of atrocious spelling is
that? And what does it mean?"

Peeved at the interruption, she kept typing and answered, "Wat
duz *WAT* mean?"

"That writing on the screen. The jargon your friends are sending you, which sounds an awful lot like the way E.T. talked in the
movie. Look—here comes some more . . . 'CU lata.' Now what
does *that* mean? Is it a new coffee flavor of some kind?"

"*No*, Mom," she answered. "It means—Oh wait a minute!" She

quickly typed in, "Brb, every1," and turned patronizingly around to me.

"UC," she began.

"Whoa! Wait a minute. Say it in English," I admonished.

"You see," she began again, "we use a different type of spelling when we chat online. It's much easier and saves time. It's pronounced the same as always, but it's quicker to type and read. For example, when I want to say, 'Be right back, everyone,' I use, 'Brb, every1,' instead. Or, I'll hit 'CU lata,' rather than type out, 'See you later.' It's a real time-saver."

"OIC," I said thoughtfully.

After observing further, I momentarily asked, "Then what about this word, 'kewl'? I assume it means, 'cool . . . ' but it has the same number of letters, either way."

"Phonetically, it makes more sense," she explained. "Why waste time using some English linguist's twist on the alphabet, when 'kewl' comes off the fingers more naturally?"

"Hmm," I mused. "I wonder what your second grade teacher would think about that . . ."

"Oh, you mean Mrs. Jonz?"

"No—I mean Mrs. *Jones*," I corrected. "She took great care in teaching you how to spell words like, 'about,' 'until,' 'know,' 'better,' and 'nothing.' Yet for all of her efforts, you're sending e-mail messages like this one: 'Dear Ashley: Can't tell U any more bout that cute kid in our class till I no something. Betta go now; nuttin more to say—Me.' "

Looking down at her hands poised on the keyboard, I expected her eyes to start showing some chagrin. Instead, she had them trained on the computer monitor and an incoming response from Ashley. "Waz up?" it read. "Got your message but g2g now, as sorta have gobs of homework. Talk 2U lata, KK?"

"G2g . . . ? " I started to ask.

"Got to go!" my daughter answered, typing feverishly.

"O," I said. "And I suppose 'KK' means, 'OK.' "

"Ya."

"Isn't that rather babyish? Don't you remember the months we spent teaching you how to talk? Have you no appreciation for what you're undoing here?"

Before I could continue my lecture, the instant-messaging box we'd been using to "I.M." Ashley suddenly grew into three boxes, each with a different name attached. Then it multiplied into four, then five, and finally six.

My young e-mailer was really fervent now—reading messages from six friends simultaneously, scanning each box for pertinent news and typing in jumbles of consonants in reply. I'd never seen anything like it. There had apparently been a prearranged log-on time, which all seven friends honored unconditionally. Clearly, it put to shame the previous generation's system of passing around an in-class note that read, "Everyone meet at the swing-set after school so we can all talk."

I could see why she abbreviated. This was like playing Bingo with six cards at once. Except that these girls could type faster than any Bingo announcer could shout numbers.

Cross-eyed from reading and deciphering incoming messages from all parts of the city, I finally closed my eyelids and rubbed them hard, walking away.

And I thought my three-way calling telephone service was the ultimate in communication. Obviously, I didn't know what "ultimate" really was.

Now all I need is an adult education course that teaches this new, "shoddy-spell" e-mail language to floundering parents. If I find one, I'll sign up in a heartbeat.

. . . And b betta off 4 it, I'm shur.

CINDY KAUFFMAN

FREEWAY OF LOVE

I *rolled my new pre-owned car home from the lot and* phoned my stepbrother Phil across the California border in Nevada.

"I'm getting rid of the Civic," I told him. "It's yours." Phil drove an Accord whose odometer had rolled over twice. I figured he could use reliable wheels that had traveled only 100,000 miles.

"No thanks," he said. "My Honda's running fine."

"Phil," I persisted, "you don't have to buy it. It's a gift. I owe you a vehicle."

Phil had bought a '74 Dodge pickup the year before we graduated from our Massachusetts high school. My mother had married his dad not long before and had moved her three children in with her new husband's four.

In a house with seven kids, thrift was king and cars were purchased used, never new. The town was semi-rural then, and it was as common for a teenager to have his or her own car as it was to pose for a yearbook picture. We step-kids' ages overlapped so most of us attended high school at the same time, which meant that our driveway was a jumble of rusty maternal station wagons parked next to teen-envy vans with shag-carpeted interiors. My stepfather's agreement to co-sign Phil's new car loan, representing a departure from family culture, demonstrated faith in Phil and his future.

In 1977, Phil got behind the wheel of that future, drove the Dodge west, and found a permanent parking spot in Nevada.

The next year I followed and settled in San Francisco. Every few months he took the pickup to the Bay Area to visit me.

"Don't you remember what happened?" I reminded Phil now. During one of those visits, he loaned me the truck. While I cruised at 55 miles per hour in Interstate 80's slow lane, a flatbed pulled in front of me from a shoulder stop. I skidded and rear ended the flatbed and spun 360 degrees, wrecking Phil's pickup.

"That was long ago," Phil said. "You do not owe me a car."

Yes, I owe you, I thought. *I'm compulsive about repaying debts and now, finally, I have the means to settle this one. No way I'll accept your refusal.*

Before my mother married Phil's dad, the only stepfamily our parents knew was the Brady Bunch. On television, conflicts got resolved in thirty minutes, minus commercials. Bunk beds blend a family, the newlyweds decided. Meanwhile, we stepchildren circled each other like cats, trying to adjust to a marriage we hadn't chosen. We doubled up in bedrooms, but we functioned like seven only children tossed together rather than one unified family.

Phil and I were the independent, well-behaved middle children. We showed up for school, turned in homework. I baked double batches of Toll House cookies. Phil mowed the lawn. We got our chores done and came home on time. We avoided both shining at science and getting in trouble, activities that would call attention to us.

Then one day, after Phil finished raking and bagging, he joined me in the kitchen, where he nibbled steaming cookies and gulped milk.

"Um, good. Thanks," he said, lingering. Baking was my job and thanks were unexpected. Plus, we more co-existed than lived together. I expected Phil to grab a snack and hide in his bedroom with the stereo cranked, not to keep me company and throw in a compliment.

Phil and I became buddies. He had a motorcycle that he seemed to disembowel at least once a month, diagnosing a problem only he could detect, then reassembling it bit by greasy bit. On summer afternoons, I sat on the driveway while he connected the nest of wires. After he kick started it I put on the second helmet and climbed behind, leaning with him into the curves as we cooled ourselves in the wind's air conditioning.

When he traded the motorbike for the pickup, I helped him buff it to a high shine. We pulled on cutoffs, loaded a rowboat and a cooler in the back, and drove to the nearby lake. We took turns pulling oars and lathering on suntan lotion. At the lake's center where the depth turned the water ebony, we dove in and floated on our backs, gazing at the lazy sky.

In our family, the girls' curfews were stricter than the boys'. If I shouted, "I'm going out with Elena," Mom answered, "Be home by ten." My stepfather paced the sleepless hallways until each teen's car was parked neatly in the driveway. But our parents warmed to the camaraderie Phil and I shared. If the two of us headed to the neighborhood hangout together, Mom let me stay out until eleven and my stepfather went to bed trusting that we'd look after each other.

Phil and I never talked about what drew us together, but we had plenty in common. We'd each lost a parent in the days before bereavement counseling and we stifled our feelings, even from ourselves. We moved cheerily into our parents' second marriage, like refugees after a war no one can explain. Then, at the eye of our unwieldy clan's cyclone, we blended into the background.

Although neither of us could express the loss buried deeper than that summer lake's center, I think now that we understood each other. Phil reached toward me when I didn't know I was sinking. And instead of diving in to contemplate the water's bottomless darkness, I resurfaced and found a friend splashing beside me. We may not have known consciously that we were quietly troubled. But our companionship assured us, gently, that we would survive.

Now I offered Phil a car and he refused. How, then, would I compensate him for the demolished vehicle?

I thought back to the phone call when I told Phil I'd totaled his treasured truck.

"Phil, I have bad news. I got in an accident." I heard him suck in a breath.

"Were you hurt?"

"Phil, the truck's totaled."

"I asked, were you hurt?"

"No."

"That's all that matters," he said.

And I realized that crashing Phil's pickup didn't put me in his debt. Loving him did. And giving him a car wouldn't even my balance sheet. I'd owe Phil for the rest of my life.

And this was an obligation that, finally, I would never want to be rid of.

LYSSA FRIEDMAN

VI
WHY ME?

Life is always either a tightrope or a feather bed.
Give mc the tightrope.

EDITH WHARTON

THE LONG RUN

I *would kill her for this. The girl had no morals at all.*
I banged on the door, then scrambled for cover when the
outside light flashed on. Locked out of my own house on
New Year's Eve and wearing nothing but a scowl, I crouched into
the corner of the carport, pressing myself as far into the shadow
as possible. My naked back flinched against the cold metal handle
of the lawn mower, and I wondered for the hundredth time how I
got into these situations when my cousin and I were together.

Stacy had always had a persuasive influence over me and, even
now that we were both eighteen years old, she could still cajole
me into doing things with her that she didn't have the guts to do
on her own. She had turned on the stereo so loud that the dog
next door began to howl along with the Eagles. A breeze whipped
around me, and I hugged my body with my arms and bounced
back and forth to the reverberating beat of the album, my bare
feet pattering against the icy concrete.

I could say a lot of things about Stacy, not the least of which
was that she had style. I knew that she would let me in, thank you
very much, right at midnight to the sound of honking horns so
we could welcome in the New Year with pizzazz. I almost
laughed, reflecting on how I had come to be shivering my tail off.

We'd just spent an hour sincerely laboring over a list of resolutions. They included some of the usual promises: exercise every
day, wash the dishes after every meal, take a vitamin pill every
morning, and organize all our pictures into photo albums—an almost overwhelming task since we had grocery bags and shoe

boxes overflowing with mementos. Our list also included some more difficult resolutions: we were going to try never to say anything nasty about anyone, never cuss around someone it might offend, and never kiss guys we didn't like just to get them to go away. We had finished at about a quarter to midnight and had fifteen minutes before our lives would change forever.

Instead of feeling good and self-righteous, I felt like a little girl again, wearing a stiff lacy dress and tight shoes, waiting on a hard, thin cushioned, church bench. A suffocating feeling of too much goodness dissolved when Stacy said, "Let's streak around the house!"

Responding to my "you're crazy" look, she implored, "Come on. It's dark. No one will see us. We'll be back inside within two minutes, and, besides, we have to do something special before midnight."

Now shivering in the corner of the carport, I wondered what had emboldened me to strip down to my birthday suit and follow Stacy out the door. Having been independent and poor for the past seven months since graduating from high school, I still feared the "real world" and wasn't sure how I would come to fit into it. I was busy with the pressures of my first full-time job and missed my frequent walks in the woods. Standing out in the crisp night air with a soft, cool wind caressing my body, I had to admit that our naked run had been out of the ordinary and kind of special. Not that I needed to prolong it for much longer.

My cousin's motivation for streaking was vastly different. Stacy had a blend of insecurities and self-confidence and seemed to believe the world was created for her to have fun. But nature was not her cup of tea; she was squeamish about almost anything not found in a mall. No, feeling the air against her slender body and the damp grass on her bare toes was not her primary reason for this escapade. Under the pressures of being popular in her senior class, just being able to totally relax and be herself was a refreshing change for Stacy.

So, dismissing my insecurities, I had yanked off my sweatshirt and frayed patched jeans as Stacy carefully removed her designer slacks and polo shirt. Then, giggling, we removed our bras and panties.

I peered intently out the window to make sure none of the neighbors happened to be outside, and solemnly said, "Okay, the coast is clear."

She took a deep breath and darted out with me right behind her. We ran as fast as we could in the dark, but the action took place in slow motion. Passing the clothesline pole, I stepped on a soft anthill, then into the patch of light that poured from my bedroom window. I could see into the window of the house behind mine where my elderly landlord and his wife were watching television. I wanted to yell with the joy of being young and alive and outside instead of shuffling around in a stuffy house with little lace doilies everywhere.

Stacy beat me back to the door by several seconds. As she skittered up the two steps, I heard her laugh and, in a horrible flash, I knew the idea that had hit her.

"Don't you dare!" I yelled as I dashed behind her and flung open the screen door just as the wooden door slammed shut in my face.

I was naked and cold but unable to stop the flow of warm feelings for my cousin. She had barred me from my own home, but had also given me a gift of feeling that the world belonged to me as much as to anyone. A delicious sense of freedom enveloped me.

As the bell at the university rang the first of twelve peals, the lock clicked and the door slowly opened. Stacy peeked around it in mischievous triumph mixed with concern. She looked relieved when I smiled, and she turned off the porch light so I could slink into the house. I gratefully snuggled into my robe that she had warmed over the radiator.

She had been busy in the kitchen. On the table were a bag of corn chips, an open can of bean dip, and a book of matches. We each dunked a chip into the dip and clicked them together to toast the new year, then we took our resolutions to the sink and set them on fire as Don Henley sang about who will come out in the end, ". . . We'll find out in the long run."

APRIL BURK

I want to be an optimist but I don't think it's going to work out.
Author unknown

BABY-SITTING NIGHTMARE

When I was twelve, my parents let me baby-sit for Mr. and Mrs. Joseph who lived down the street with their two little preschool girls. It was summertime, and most of my baby-sitting occurred during daylight hours while Mrs. Joseph went shopping or played bridge with her friends.

Then she asked if I could stay with her daughters in the evening, promising she and her husband would be home by ten P.M. After I begged and pleaded, desperate to earn fifty cents an hour for six hours—three whole dollars!—my parents agreed.

At four o'clock, I knocked on the Josephs' front door, greeted the kids, and received detailed instructions from their mother. A few minutes later, the girls and I were alone. We played hide-and-seek, did some finger painting together, and I fixed them scrambled eggs and toast soldiers for an early dinner. Then, as the colors of a summer sunset splashed across the sky at about eight P.M., I gathered the two little towheads beside me on the couch in front of the picture window and began to read them a story.

I heard a soft click, as if the front door had been opened, and I paused.

"Go on," said Melanie, the four-year-old. "Keep reading."

"Wait." I put my finger to my lips, and her eyes grew huge as I whispered, "I thought I heard someone come in."

I heard the click again, and the lamp beside me switched on. All three of us jumped. Then the drapes closed across the big window.

I screamed, grabbed a little girl under each of my arms, and ran upstairs to the bathroom. As I slammed and locked the door behind us, I heard rock and roll music begin to play from a radio somewhere downstairs.

The girls wiggled and squealed then clutched each other in abject fear as I hushed them, saying, "There's a bad man in the house. You have to be perfectly quiet."

The three of us sat on the floor, ears pressed to the wooden door . . . listening. Even two-year-old Tricia was very, very quiet. For two hours we listened to the music playing, but we never heard another sound. No footsteps, no creaking doors, no rattling of silver or breaking of china. Definitely no one walking up the stairs.

Then the front door opened with a bang—and we all jumped. Both girls leaped into my arms and the three of us trembled until we heard Mrs. Joseph call, "Peggy? Where are you?"

Melanie and Tricia and I burst out of the bathroom and ran downstairs. The girls hurled themselves against their astonished parents' legs, babbling about "bad men in the house."

In the middle of my garbled explanation, Mr. and Mrs. Joseph exchanged a look and began laughing. Then Mr. Joseph explained that he had purchased one of the first automatic timing devices ever made, and he'd rigged it to close the electric drapes and to turn on a light and a radio at sunset on nights when they went out.

"I guess I just switched it on automatically when we left tonight. Honestly, I don't even remember doing it," he explained. He apologized all over himself while Mrs. Joseph went upstairs to very belatedly put the girls to bed.

Mr. Joseph walked me six houses up the street to my house and handed me not the three dollars that I expected, but five dollars. I stared at it and wondered if I should protest, if I ought to refuse the overpayment. But then I folded the money in a little wad and tucked it in my pocket.

"Good night," I said as he turned to walk home, "and thanks."

Five whole dollars was just about right, I figured, as payment for being scared out of my wits.

PEGGY VINCENT

It's the good girls who keep the diaries;
the bad girls never have the time.
TALLULAH BANKHEAD

FOREVER EYES

If you've ever pulled the wings off a butterfly, you
know how I feel each time I remember that reckless night
when I held power and cruelty in my hands. A moment to do
what I would . . . and then remember forever. We were a gang
that ordinary night, Betty, Sandy, Rosie, and I. With slicked down
DA haircuts and matching Bermuda shorts almost covered by our
dads' discarded white shirts, we were the country-club version of
"bad." Not bad in the sense of wild lawbreakers or sexy little thrill
seekers. Just bad as in cool, and out for an evening of pizza and
fun. In the beginning, anyway.

How old were we then? I know one of us was old enough
to drive. That's how we got from our tidy, two-story suburban
homes to these trash-strewn streets of the inner city. The nearest
any of us came to a real gang was Rosie, one of five kids. Betty had
some little brothers, and Sandy and I were each an only child. All
of us were pampered, well fed, and mostly ignored at home, as
long as we stayed on the honor roll and minded our manners.

Maybe it was the movies, perhaps the books. We'd all seen
Blackboard Jungle and read *A Stone for Danny Fisher*. There was a certain, unadmitted romance in tough girls and swaggering guys. Of

all the Little Golden Books in our childhood, we hadn't yet read
Lord of the Flies.

There was no plan, the night just evolved around us and we
around it. Armored with heavy makeup and tough talk, we felt
ourselves strong. We became the stories we read and merged into
one movie-screen-size entity from a concrete jungle. With gold-
tipped Egyptian cigarettes stuck between Revlon red lips, we
rolled our hips and swaggered along the avenue past noisy bars
and neon-bright diners. Guys hooted and called and we yelled
back with confident disdain. We were mean; we were cool.

We looked so good. Rosie had her frizzy red hair pulled back on
one side like Rita Hayworth. Sandy wore big hoop earrings and,
like me, she had a bleached blonde streak in her dark hair. Always
an attention-getter, Betty's bobbling breasts pointed the way.
Stuffed with socks, my own bra helped me belong. Shoulders
back, chests out, we marched forward, shimmering shadows of
the future us. At that moment, I had no clue how much an un-
guarded deed could sour tomorrow's memories.

The red and blue lights of Jerry's pizzeria beckoned.

"You wanna?"

"Sure."

We sauntered into the half-filled restaurant and looked around.
Four girls occupied one table. Many others were empty. We ap-
proached the girls' table, then stopped. With hands on hips, Rosie
said, "I believe you're sitting at our table."

"Says who?" The fat girl pushed back a sauce-smeared plate and
wiped her greasy cheek. "You chicks looking for trouble, you
found it." Three tough faces sneered at us.

Sandy reached out and jerked the edge of their table. A drink
spilled.

Chairs screeched as the girls jumped up.

"Hey, hey," yelled the short dark man. "Youse get outta my
place. Don't makea no trouble here. G'wan, out! Now, or I call da
cops."

One of the girls reached into her jeans and threw a dollar tip on the table. "It's okay, Jerry. We're leaving. No problem."

The fat girl glared at us and said, "What? We just gonna let them get away with this?"

A tall, mahogany-hued girl grabbed Fatty's arm. "C'mon, Juanita. We don't need no more hassles with the cops. We're done anyway. Let's go."

After they left, we sat down at a clean table across the room. Before the waiter came over, Betty leaned forward, "What do you think, shall we?"

We all looked at one another, then stood up in silent decision.

Rumble, I thought. A good movie word, but scary in truth. The street outside belonged to those girls. They were the tough ones; we were just wanna-be's. What if one of them had a switchblade? But—afraid to show fear—I followed everyone out the door.

There they were, on the far side of the cindered parking lot, grouped together and looking back at us in expectation. We— The Beast—walked toward them, no weapons but our hands. Betty began to chuckle.

"All right, ladies," she said. "Pick your victim."

I cannot recall the full battle scene from this far forward. I was in my own very private world, spiraling down to a place I never thought to be.

The girl I fought was built much like me, but her scrawny, thin bones were no match for my red-hot elation. Quickly, I had her pinned down on the asphalt. I straddled her, then sat hard on her hips. I grabbed her chest, pulled up a handful of shirt and bra, then paused. My bunched-up fist held her secret. Like me, she stuffed her bra. Here was a sister of my soul. Another skinny kid trying to get along with the endowed others. Only we knew what it was to be a bag of bones and a hank of hair, to feel woebegone boards where soft plumpness should be. Others were wearing B-cup bras, some already in C-cups, while we languished in the demitasse-cup world of an eleven-year-old.

This girl on the ground—her secret angered me. Our eyes met and held. For one forever moment I melted into her eyes and looked back at myself. Strobe lights of pity and fury pulsated forward and back. I felt her fear and begged myself for compassion.

Her lips whispered, "Don't. Oh, please. Don't."

Fright and shame swirled in her eyes, then converged to humiliated horror as I gave one mighty yank. Old socks rolled out onto the ground and a certain light left her eyes.

Instantly, I jumped up and left her there, like a fallen, crippled deer, and ran back to my own herd. One leap over the parking lot fence and we were gone.

No one found out. No ax ever fell and we never spoke of the incident. But—like a persistent little mouse—a gnawing ache chews deep in my heart when I remember my cruelty to that girl. Her eyes forever remind me to have a conscience in everything.

LYNNE LAYTON ZIELINSKI

LOST AND FOUND

I truly don't know what caused me to fall for Chris. When I was a little girl, Chris was like a brother, the cute boy next door as we rode the yellow bus to school. Whatever it was that caused me to shift my thinking about him years later insured me a tumultuous eighth-grade year.

My problems began in sixth period life science class. My best friend, America, and I were whispering together. I told her how I felt about Chris, describing him as a tall, dark, and mysteriously handsome athlete.

Jokingly, she wrote, "I love C.H." on my hand in permanent blue ink.

I knew I needed to wash it off. To make matters worse, Melinda, a very popular girl in school, grabbed my hand and shouted out the first thing that came out of her pea-size brain.

"Melissa loves Chris!"

Everyone in the room stopped what they were doing in shocked silence. You could have heard a pin drop. A moment later, everybody went back to his or her conversations. But, all was not forgotten.

Later, in pre-algebra, I took a back row seat because I was really shy and hated to be called on in class. I had just settled in my chair when Chris walked by me, turned around and said, "Hey, Melissa, I heard you have a crush on me, huh?"

"No," I replied, blushing.

"Yeah, if you don't like me, why are you blushing?"

Fortunately for me the bell rang and class started.

This was the start of an extremely embarrassing and painful run of events. First, a note written by one of my well-intentioned friends appeared in Chris's locker, telling him he'd been cruel to me. Then, I was mocked and ridiculed by the popular girls at a school dance. To top that off, I received a note in *my* locker from some seventh-grade girl threatening me to stay away from "her man Chris"! If that wasn't enough, one of Chris's friends "accidentally" spilled his milk all over me in the cafeteria. And last (but not least), our misguided but well-meaning science teacher partnered me with Chris for a month and a half during a lab assignment.

I was truly regretting ever having set foot into the "liking boys" territory. I clung to the hope that maybe this whole affair would fade to the background . . . until *the note*.

Chris received a note with a rose, supposedly from me, just before the Valentine's dance. It read something dopey like: "I've never found someone as sexy as you." Of course, I was blamed and shamed once again. I ran into the bathroom and sat down and cried into the coats of my friends who knew I would never put myself that low. I stayed there for the first two periods that day and cursed boys, life, and whoever put that note on his locker. We never did find out who did it.

Now that I look back on that agonizing year, I'm truly grateful for Chris doing things exactly as he did. I believe that if he had treated me with respect, I still would be shy today. Because of all the unwanted attention I received, I sought a way to get myself out of town to forget about what had happened.

I took a three week trip to Europe with the People to People program, and in the process, met and had fun with a tall, dark, and handsome athlete from another state. And I made many other friends who I'm still in touch with today.

Although Chris tortured me and ultimately made my life miserable during my eighth-grade year, something wonderful came from the experience. Instead of retreating into my shell, I broke out of it and became more outgoing in ways I never would have imagined possible.

Now in high school, ironically, I still count Chris as one of the most important guy friends in my life. To this day, he still teases me about that fateful year, and I tease him back. Many people tell me that he wouldn't have tortured me unless he felt somewhat the same way about me. Some even venture to say that one day we will be married. I don't know about that—only time will tell.

What I do know is that something good came from all the agony. My despair led me to Europe. I must admit that in the beginning I may not have signed up for the trip for all the right reasons. I was lost and wanted to escape. In the end, though, it was exactly what I needed. For it was in the getting-away that I found a whole new world—and along with it, a whole new me.

MELISSA GREENE

*Learn to get in touch with silence within yourself
and know that everything in this life has a purpose.
There are no mistakes, no coincidences,
all events are blessings given to us to learn from.*
ELISABETH KÜBLER-ROSS

THE OTHER PRIZE

The speech competition promised a great prize—
a chance at a sizable college scholarship. And in my
junior year in high school, figuring out how to pay for
college had jumped to the top of my priority list. I wrote a speech
and was surprised when I won the local, district, and zone levels of
the contest, bringing me to the state competition, the second to
last step before the national event, where scholarship dollars were
awarded.

I practiced daily, honing my presentation in front of my
mom, the mirror, and the dog. The speech I wrote was about
the future for youth in America. My heart was pounding when
I delivered my ten minutes of prose. I was nervous, but the
words came out flawlessly, and I knew I had done well. My
teacher/coach gave me an excited thumbs-up as I left the stage
and took my seat.

When I returned to the stage with the other competitors

for the awards presentation a few minutes later, I was sure I'd at
least take second place. For me, second was good enough—the
first and second place winners went on to the national competition and won considerably higher cash prizes than the other
finalists.

One by one, the prizes were awarded. Fourth place was given
to a girl from a nearby school, third to a boy who shook as he accepted his trophy and check.

"Second place goes to Shirley Kawa," said the announcer. I
stepped forward and he handed me a huge trophy and a nice
check.

I sat back down, applauded the girl who won first place, and
started dreaming of the next leg of the competition.

Before the applause died down, another man came running up
on stage. "Wait, there's been a mistake," he said.

To my horror, and in front of two hundred people, he walked
over to me, yanked away my trophy and check, and then handed
them to the boy beside me. "I'm sorry," he whispered. "But he's a
boy. He'll need it more."

This wasn't the 1950s—it was the twentieth century and girls
were succeeding as much as their male counterparts. But the
contest was run by a staunchly male organization and maybe that
was why they'd decided two girls were one too many. I sat there,
stunned, as the man exchanged the boy's third place trophy with
me and then left the stage.

My chances for a scholarship drained away, replaced by a humiliation so strong it felt like needles against my skin. I wanted
to burst into tears, to throw a tantrum and stalk off the stage. But
I bit back the tears, swallowed the lump in my throat, and stilled
my shakes. I stood there with the other finalists, a smile cemented
onto my lips, as the audience clapped. I hated every interminable
second that passed.

My coach and I protested afterward, but the score sheets had already been redone to reflect the new ranking, erasing the previous scores. There was nothing we could do. We went home with a strong sense of injustice riding in the backseat.

I competed halfheartedly the next year, winning only the local and district levels. Then I gave up and bowed out at zone, afraid to even shoot for state again. The fear was nearly crippling, keeping me from all other speech competitions. For years, I thought of that day with anger, sure that it had cost me the funds for a "good" college. I may have acted graciously that day, yet I felt anything but.

It took me a long time—years, actually—to realize that as humiliating as the loss was, I learned a very important lesson. Being a good student, I hadn't hit many obstacles or snags along the way through school. A's came easily and I was somewhat cocky and overly confident.

That moment on stage lives in the back of my mind as a constant reminder that sometimes life is unfair. Being good at something doesn't automatically make you a winner. And one horrible moment can change you—for the better.

I left a lot of my cockiness back in the auditorium that day. And ironically, I gained a richer, more authentic sense of self-confidence and determination, with time. One organization, and its opinion that a girl wasn't entitled to the same perks as a boy, wasn't going to beat me.

As I got older, the competition grew stiffer. I worked through college, paying my own way. My days became a roller coaster of triumphs and setbacks. It never lasted long, though. Whenever I experienced a disappointment, I'd think back to that day on the stage when I had my prize literally ripped out of my hands and given to someone else because of his gender. Success is not just about being the best. It's about persevering, even in the face of adversity.

I spent the check a long time ago. The trophy is somewhere

in the attic, gathering dust. But the lessons of that day have been lifelong: Learning to lose graciously is sometimes the best way to win.

SHIRLEY KAWA-JUMP

THE GENERATION GAP
IS ALIVE AND WELL

*I*t seems to me that the criteria for employment in a bookstore should be more stringent than looking funky, cool, and groovy. The infant in the bookstore who asked if he could assist me sported a chain from his nostril to his earlobe, his hair stood on end in spikes, his baggy pants revealed a fashionable amount of his boxers, and his fingernails were painted black.

Hard to imagine that he might just set someone's heart ablaze. Scary to think that heart might belong to one of my nieces, lovely young ladies whose heads aren't so easily turned. Oh no.

Now I appreciate the Goth look just as much as the next middle-aged woman does. If the clerk knows his job, it doesn't matter to me how many of his body parts are pierced and tattooed.

I requested a copy of *Walden*.

"Who wrote that?" he asked, staring at the computer monitor.

"Henry David Thoreau."

"Never heard of the dude. Spell that out for me," he requested.

"H-E-N . . ." I began.

"No," he interrupted. "I've got that part. Spell his last name. I can't find him in the computer. I think this *Walden* is out of print. It was probably written before 1997."

I made a mental note to myself to go to the public library and take the girls with me. There's really no need for them to fritter away their time browsing the bookstore aisles.

I asked him to show me CDs of Welsh music. He told me to go look in the Eastern Europe section and returned to the phone he'd pulled from his pocket. Eavesdropping I heard, "Yeah . . . (low laughter) . . . yeah . . . (low laughter)."

I studied his tattoos while waiting for a break in the conversation. I read his nametag, "Shane. Happy to help." He clasped the receiver to his chest and returned my stare. "Yeah?" he challenged.

I pinned him with an icy glare. "Wales is not in Eastern Europe."

"Yeah?"

I was sorely tempted to say "yeah" but I replied, "That's correct." At his blank stare, I elaborated. "Wales is part of the United Kingdom." This was no time to be meek so I tried a final stab at piercing the darkness. "You know . . . England?"

"Uh, try the Eastern Europe section." He returned to the phone.

Thinking he just might have a creative shelving system, I actually went over to peruse CDs from Uzbekistan and parts east, glancing at performers whose names I couldn't pronounce. I swiftly concluded he *was* as dumb as he looked.

When all else failed, I checked the offerings on the Internet and selected a CD of a Welsh men's chorus. After the order was placed, the company let me in on their dirty little secret—the order would take *weeks* to arrive. I suspect the dudes at the Internet company ordered it from the United Kingdom (you know . . . England?).

I regaled everyone at our next family gathering with the details of my futile shopping trip to the bookstore—the clerk's ineptness, his dramatic appearance, and my frustration. We old fogies clucked our tongues and wondered what this world was coming to. But three pretty heads swiveled in my direction, then turned to one another. "Shane," they cooed. "Ooh!"

"Shane?" I repeated. The stars in their eyes confirmed my worst suspicions. I'm a relic of the 1900s and definitely not with it. I smiled weakly at my nieces but thought to myself—eww.

LANA ROBERTSON HAYES

LESS IS MORE

We had just spent a great weekend with our grandchildren. We played at the park and worked on crafts until, tired out, they settled in the living room watching a favorite Disney movie while their grandfather relaxed in his lounge chair.

While preparing dinner, I checked occasionally on the chicken browning on the rotisserie. What a wonderful aroma. I breathed it in. Stopped. Sniffed the air again. What was that other familiar smell? Mixed in with that of the chicken, it was difficult to tell. I moved into the dining room. The odor, now stronger, was more familiar. Checking in the living room, I found my hubby dozing in the recliner and our grandson flopped on his stomach in front of the television. I quickly scanned the room. Our five-year-old granddaughter was suspiciously absent.

Following the ever-increasing scent, I found her in the master bedroom, surrounded by a haze of my best perfume. As I entered, a look of "Oops, busted" crossed her face and she scurried to the dresser, pushing the bottle back against the mirror with a re-sounding clunk.

"Sorry, Grandma," she said, her expression most serious as she observed my raised eyebrows. "But . . . I . . . I . . . *really* like your perfume."

I sighed, waving my hands in an effort to disperse the over-powering scent. "I like it too," I said, "but with some things less is more, and perfume is one of them."

She wrinkled her nose. "Less is more?"

Laughing, I settled on the bed and patted the spot beside me. "Sit here and I'll explain."

She climbed up, leaning against me as I began . . .

"When I was a teenager, I, like many young women, became concerned with how I looked. You see, I had a boyfriend and wanted to impress him." My granddaughter giggled and cuddled closer.

"I practiced putting on my makeup. Mother would watch and remind me, 'Less is more, Christine, less is more.' And although Mother wore only lipstick, she explained about using makeup to enhance, not overpower. A little lipstick shows the shape of the mouth. A little eye shadow makes the eyes look larger and brighter. But if you put on lots of red lipstick, guck your eyes up with eye shadow and layers of mascara, and give yourself big red cheeks, you'll look like . . ."

"A clown," my granddaughter interjected.

"Yes a clown. And we knew a lady who wore rouge like a clown, and I didn't want people laughing at me like they did at her. So you would think that I had learned what less is more meant, wouldn't you?

"However, still dissatisfied with my appearance, I decided to bleach my hair. Then I had it permed. My dry hair looked like the Scarecrow's in *The Wizard of Oz*. I was frantic. The next day I was going to meet my boyfriend's brother and sister-in-law. How could I go looking like this?

"Mother calmed me down. When she was a girl, she said, they rubbed Vaseline into the dry ends of hair to soften it. Desperate, I decided to give it a try.

"That evening, I rubbed a small amount of Vaseline into my ends and they felt much better. I ran my hands over the rest of the hair. Dry as cornflakes. Did I dare use more Vaseline? I hesitated. But if a little worked so well on the ends, a lot would soften the rest, I reasoned. Yes. With a firm resolve, I scooped out a handful of Vaseline, rubbed it between my hands, and worked it through my hair. It made my hair sticky. I ran a comb through it. The hair hung stiff and straight as though starched. I thought I would wrap a towel around it for the night, rinse out the grease in the morning, and bingo, I'd have soft, beautiful hair. Convinced of this, I climbed into bed, towel securely in place.

"The next morning, I found the towel had slipped from my head and there was a huge greasy spot on my pillow. I'd have to wash the pillowcase before Mother saw it or I'd really be in the soup, so I stripped it from the pillow and shoved it under my bed. I'd worry about that later, after my hair, which was glued to the side of my face, was soft and beautiful again.

"In the bathroom, I shampooed and towel-dried my hair. It still felt sticky, so I shampooed it again. And again. And again. Then I shrieked for Mother. What was I to do? My date was coming early and I couldn't go anywhere looking like this. I showed her my hair hanging in greasy strings.

"She shook a finger at me. 'How many times have I told you, Christine,' she said, 'less is more.'

"Tears sprang to my eyes. Couldn't she see my predicament? The last thing I needed was a lecture. Seeing my misery, she put her arm around my shoulders, giving me a squeeze. Then she left the bathroom, returning with a bar of soap and a jug of vinegar.

"I don't remember how many washings it took with that bar of laundry soap, or how many rinses with vinegar, but eventually my hair was presentable. With little time left before my date arrived, I pulled my hair into a simple, damp ponytail. It wasn't how I had envisioned it, but it was better than a head of Vaseline. And my boyfriend's family was gracious and never once questioned the faint odor of vinegar that followed wherever I went."

My granddaughter giggled as I squeezed her hand and asked, "Now do you understand what 'less is more' means?"

"Yup," she said, sliding from the bed. "Let's eat. I'm hungry."

I set the table, then watched with satisfaction as the meal was enjoyed.

"Grandma," our eight-year-old grandson asked for the second time, "can I have some more chicken?"

Scowling, his sister shook her finger at him. "Don't you know, less is more?" she stated with the conviction of one who's sure of her facts. Then she looked at me and laughed, satisfied that she'd put one over on her big brother. I laughed too. No, she hadn't quite understood what less is more meant. But that was okay. I smiled at the long ago memory. Neither had I . . . to begin with.

CHRIS MIKALSON

BACKSEAT BLUES

"Tony, if you throw one more thing at me you are going to your room," I said through clenched teeth, straining to stay calm.

His four-year-old laughter filled my ears and I lost all thought of the novel I was trying to read. He devilishly danced around me while scrunching up his nose, mimicking a cartoon character he had seen on TV. His light brown bowl-cut hair swung back and forth as he moved.

How am I going to make it through a thirteen-hour car ride, sharing the backseat with him?" I wondered.

Lately, I had asked myself this a lot. Our family had planned a vacation to San Francisco, which was to begin in a matter of hours.

I need to get a good night's rest because tomorrow morning will be no picnic, I thought as he shoved a toy truck in my face.

The next morning I was ripped from a sound sleep as my brother bounced on my waterbed, landing on top of my stomach.

"Wake up! It is five, six, seven o'clock!" Tony shouted as I began to feel the effects of my simulated earthquake.

Why not? We were going to California; I might as well get used to being shaken awake. I groped around trying to get dressed and thanked the lord we had packed the car last night. Ten minutes later, I clambered into the car and gave a last glance to my dog, who was watching me with inquisitive eyes.

"Send out the distress signals by tomorrow!" I felt like screaming after I looked next to me to see my space overrun with a stack of pillows, a cooler, a bag of toys brimming to the top, and my brother.

Twelve hours and forty-five minutes to go, I reminded myself. Sure thing.

After dozing off and awakening several times to my brother's bothersome chatter, I was ready to give up on trying to sleep.

"Color with me!" Tony said.

"I can't, Tony, it will make me carsick if I do."

"Then you don't love me!" he said as tears filled up his eyes.

He is so irritating! I couldn't figure out why everyone in grocery store lines, on the playground, or at first glance falls in love with Tony. They don't know any better because they don't live with him.

I held back feelings of nausea and started the task of coloring a picture of Batman flying through the air. *It could be worse,* I told myself, but I definitely was not in a positive state of mind. At least he wouldn't be able to tear up my room for a couple of weeks. That brought me some comfort.

After what seemed like an eternity, we arrived. I had been struck with plastic toys and weathered a handful of insults, but I made it to the first stop of our trip. Now I could go to bed; unfortunately for me, shared with his truly.

This ought to be a thrill in the making, I thought sarcastically.

My friend Lizzie would have said, "Oh joy and rapture," if she were here. Actually, I only ended up locking myself in the closet once that night to get away from him.

The next morning, we went to the beach. None of us had our swimsuits, but after sticking my feet in the chilly water I decided I really couldn't care less. This was not good water temperature for swimming. It was certainly not like the pools and lakes at home.

"Take your brother in the water, Rachael!" My father yelled from across the beach.

It figured I would get stuck watching him again. Built-in babysitters don't exactly get time off, even during vacations, I reminded myself under my breath.

I ran along as my brother squealed in delight at seeing the ocean. Knee deep in freezing water, I held fast to the back of his shirt so he wouldn't be knocked over by the waves. With his splashes and refusals to go closer to shore, I didn't have time to avoid an incoming tide before my shorts were soaked with icy water and my brother screamed bloody murder as he got drenched.

"I tried to tell you to move back, and this is exactly what happens when you don't listen! I seriously hope we have a change of clothes in the car!" I found myself saying as I picked him up and carried him back to calmer, ankle-deep water.

Then he did something unexpected. He looked up at me with his big brown eyes, gave a great big smile, and wrapped his arms around my legs in a bear hug. It warmed me even though I was cold and wet.

Slowly I took his small hand in mine and took a couple steps forward. For the first time I noticed how relaxing and beautiful the ocean waves were, and the salty air was a pleasant change from the dry desert feel of Arizona. All my impatience and frustration melted away. I guess, sometimes, having a little brother isn't so terrible after all. I know we have fought and have been ready to kill each other numerous times since the trip began, and we probably will forever . . . but I discovered what everybody else has seen when it comes to my kid brother. You just can't help but love him.

RACHAEL FEDERICO

VII
ANGELS HERE
AND THERE

It is the creative potential itself in human beings
that is the image of God.

MARY DALY

MIND GAMES

My dad left grammar school and never returned. He had to go to work to earn money so that his family could survive. But he loved reading, loved books, and loved words. He spent a lifetime studying.

It was during my high school years that the local newspaper began a word-game contest. Those who participated could have as many entries as they liked. The contest looked easy, but it was a tricky business. The words kept changing meanings and no one was winning the generous prize money.

Every Sunday my dad rushed to the corner store for the newspapers. He bought fifteen, though we certainly could not afford even ten. If I was sleeping, he would wake me. If I was talking on the telephone, he would interrupt.

"Harriet, could you help me out here for a couple minutes?"

The couple minutes usually lasted several hours. I would sit at the table surrounded by dictionaries. Then the debate would begin. If I chose a word for the blank space, I had to defend that word. I had to know not only the definition but also the intent. I had to explain why my word deserved preference over the one my father had chosen. He, too, would have a defense.

There were Sundays when we would sit at the kitchen table most of the day. Once our answers were chosen, we then carefully had to tend to the clerical work, cutting the entries from the newspaper, addressing envelopes.

As the weeks passed, I desperately wished that the contest would be canceled and I could return to Sundays with my friends.

I found it difficult to explain to potential dates that being "busy" meant working on a word-game contest with my dad. Sometimes, to put me in a better mood, my dad would take me for a special treat before we began work. But even then, the discussion centered on the contest.

"We were close this week," he'd tell me between gulps of ice cream. "We only lost by two."

It might have been two million, I thought, hoping that someone's victory would take the pressure off us.

One day, it finally happened. A winner. I also felt victorious for surely my dad would give up his quest. Instead, he just said, "Well, we know it can be done. And we're going to do it."

The contest continued for more than a year and so did we. I don't remember exactly when it stopped or when the kitchen table finally was cleared of dictionaries, newspapers, and sharpened pencils. I do know that from that year on, I looked at words differently, with more respect. I realized each word has a unique meaning that can change when added to a sentence. I learned words could fool me, but also become my friends, and if I chose, I could spend a lifetime discovering words, sharing words, and loving words.

But also, I became aware of my dad's determination, his burning passion for an education, and his desire to share the adventure of learning with me. My father and I didn't win the contest. But I walked away with the prize.

HARRIET MAY SAVITZ

Miracles are God's coups d'état.
ANNE-SOPHIE SWETCHINE

TAKE ME HOME

I was three years into anorexia and days away from death. That was according to the attending doctor of the big city hospital I was admitted to weighing a slight eighty pounds while I stood five feet seven inches tall.

My life during my early twenties had been stressful and lonely, living far from my family and having recently attended my beloved grandfather's funeral. Depriving myself of food for the past three years had been a way of keeping some sort of control of my life. It was unrealistic, unhealthy, and just plain stupid, but to me, it made some kind of sense. I had lost complete control of the disease and it now controlled me . . . and was killing me.

Upon admission to the hospital the doctors ran an array of tests. The results were grim. If I lived more than a week they would be surprised. My heart beat faintly in my chest. My electrolytes were almost completely depleted. I had zero percent body fat. I had literally starved myself to the now pending death.

I called a friend to make arrangements for my body to be sent from Texas to Wisconsin. I made it clear that my family, too far away to deal with this, was not to be told. I came to terms with the fact that my life was over. I made my peace with God, and I asked him to take me Home.

I was hooked up to heart monitors, put on oxygen, and had four IV bags hanging over me that supplied my body with antibiotics and nutritional supplements. They considered tube feeding me, but gave up on the idea when I gagged on the tube.

I continued to ask God to take me.

The nurses and doctors gave up on me. I heard one doctor talking in the hall. There would be lawsuits if they did nothing, but everything they were doing was hopeless, I could not possibly live more than a few days. "Take me Home, God," I prayed. "Let this be over." I had lost all hope of recovery and will to live, let alone wanting to go through the pains of recovery.

My mind was still alert. I had a few visitors who were horrified by my weight and the tubes and needles and beat of the heart monitor. The few came only once, it was too much for them to see. I had become a pro at dressing to hide my weight, or lack of it, and now, seeing me in the hospital gown brought reality to the surface. I wished my mind were not alert so I wouldn't feel the pain of them walking out the door with those horrified looks.

Flowers came by the dozens, and a sweet aroma filled the room. I was thankful I was not on any mind altering drugs so I could phone those I loved. I didn't tell them the truth, only that I loved them. I had no strength to write any last wishes or good-byes. I had strength enough only to pray.

After three days had passed and the city lights flooded my dark room in the middle of the night, I was suddenly hit with a familiar and pungent smell. At first I couldn't identify it, it wasn't the usual hospital smell, and it seemed to rise above the perfume smell of the now way too many flowers.

Then, with a shocking feeling, almost a fear, I recognized it. It was the smell of the wine my wonderful grandfather drank every night after dinner, served at holidays, and even let me sip when my grandmother and mother weren't looking.

Why did I smell this here, now?

I thought it was my "moment" . . . my mind was going and I was dying. I locked my hands in prayer and said, "God, I'm ready."

"No Baby Brown Eyes. It's not your time."

I swear I jumped high enough to hit my head on the ceiling. I was afraid to open my eyes. The voice was so familiar. The nickname only one person, my grandfather, had ever called me; but he had died. I slowly opened my eyes, expecting nothing, almost hoping for nothing. I was fearful I had lost my mind.

There, at the end of my cold metal hospital bed, sitting on the dull blue hospital bedspread, was my grandfather. He was not flooded in angelic light. He was not floating; he had no angel wings. He just sat there in his bib overalls and a red and blue flannel shirt.

"Grandpa, take me Home, take me with you," I pleaded urgently.

"No, it is not your time. This is not part of the plan; you must stay."

"But Grandpa, I am dying. I can't stay and I don't want to. I want this to be over," I called out more loudly than I thought I could.

"I'm sorry honey, not now. I love you, but it's not your time."

It was then that a nurse came flying through the door and switched on the light. I was almost blinded by the brightness.

I looked hopefully at the end of my bed, but Grandpa was gone.

The nurse, not in the best of moods, railed, "What the heck is all the commotion in here, and good grief, what on earth is that awful odor?" I gave her an innocent look, which made her even madder. The cranky nurse left the room and quickly returned with another, a sweeter one, who smelled the odor, too. She knew exactly what it was. She was familiar with the brand of wine.

They, not so gently, lifted my frail body into a wheelchair and removed me from the room along with my monitors and IV equipment. They stripped the bed and went through every drawer and closet, even looked in the tank of the toilet. I could hear all their bickering from outside the door where they had planted me.

Finally, after they were satisfied someone hadn't smuggled in a few bottles of wine and that I wasn't totally smashed out of my gourd, they put me back into bed. They also drew blood to do a blood alcohol level, which of course came out negative.

In the morning I was again subjected to the same battery of tests I had been given on the day of my arrival. But this time it was different. I laughed and joked with the caregivers and the needle pokers. I felt renewed and alive. I felt good. I asked for food for the first time. They looked at me funny and brought me green Jell-O. I had been thinking bacon double cheeseburger. I knew what had come over me and they wanted to know, but I wasn't about to tell them. I figured I would get locked in the loony bin and never see the light of day again if I told them, "Oh yeah, my dead grandfather came for a visit."

That evening, my doctor, looking tired, rather confused, and very anxious, came into my room. He told me to call a friend, a cab, whatever I needed to get home. He was telling me to go home!

He said he didn't know how or why, but every test came back perfectly normal—I just needed to put on weight. He said he could not explain why everything was normal. He said some called it a miracle. He did not believe in miracles. He was very clear that he wanted me out of the hospital as soon as possible. And *if* I ever was admitted again, not to ask for him.

I went home from the hospital that day with the will to start anew. I left my old ways, my worries, and my past behind. I went home and started the journey back from the grips of anorexia to receive the gift of a complete recovery.

I hold fast to that gift, I hold fast to the hand of God. And forever I will wish for my grandfather to be at the end of my bed again . . . so I can share with him all the good that has come into my life.

LINDA ASPENSON-BERGSTROM

THE BEST TEACHER EVER

Our seventh grade English teacher, Miss McHugh, was the youngest teacher we'd ever had at Public School 70. Her fluffy, brown, shoulder-length hair cascaded around her face, like Charlie's Angels on TV. Her perfume, unlike the rose water that our homeroom teacher Mrs. Bayt wore, emitted a strong and bold scent. We knew whenever she had walked down the hall moments ahead of us.

She passed our achievement test scores to us in class instead of sending them to our parents in the mail. That she thought we had the right to know how we scored before our parents did made us feel grown-up.

Walking home for lunch in early October, my best friend Nancy and I talked about the things we loved about Miss McHugh. Her bright blue eye shadow, her naturally dark eyelashes, and how she always touched our shoulders as she leaned over our desks to whisper encouraging words while we wrote poems and essays for her.

"I wonder what she does on the weekend?" I said.

"Yeah, do you think she has a boyfriend?"

"Oh definitely," I said. "I mean she must, she's so beautiful."

One Saturday morning, Nancy and I decided we would call her on the phone to see if we could discover something about her. We desperately wanted a peek into her private, after-school life. We wanted some special information, a gift of knowing her a little better than our classmates did. My parents were out, so we went into their bedroom and sat on the edge of the bed. I moved a pile of clean laundry aside and pulled out the phone book.

When Nancy found her number, we clasped arms and screamed.

I dialed, and then held the phone between our ears. I could feel Nancy's hair on my cheek and hear her breathing softly. When Miss McHugh answered, I disguised my voice, deepening it to fool her. "Speaking," she said quickly. Nancy giggled. I put the phone down and pressed it into the bed. "Shhhh!" Nancy covered her mouth with her hand, feigning seriousness.

"Who's this?" Miss McHugh asked with interest.

I froze. We hadn't planned anything past this part. We couldn't give ourselves away; she'd think we were foolish little girls, not the mature junior high scholars we wanted her to believe we were. We had to make up a name and had no time to discuss it. "Betty!" I said.

"Oh?" she said. "Betty who?"

I could hear the amusement in her voice, and I knew we weren't annoying her.

Nancy looked at the newspaper on my mother's nightstand. She pointed to a large car advertisement.

"Benz!" I almost shouted. "Betty Benz!" More muffled giggling from Nancy.

"Oh, okay." She played along. "How are you doing, Betty Benz?" I could hear the smile in her voice.

"What are you doing this weekend?" I asked. This was what we wanted. "Well," she started. "I'm going to wash my car," I pictured her forest green MG convertible sports car roaring into the school parking lot every morning, "and I'm going to a movie tonight."

That last bit sent us over the edge with giddiness. Nancy and I looked at each other and opened our mouths in a mock scream. Was it a date, or just a friend? I wanted to ask, but suddenly I was afraid that if I talked much more, she'd figure out who it really was.

"Well, goodbye!" I blurted and slammed down the phone. Nancy and I let out the shrieks we had been stifling and jumped around the room.

I hadn't thought about Miss McHugh in years. Just recently, when Nancy and her husband and children visited my family for a long weekend, I dragged out our junior high school class photo to show Nancy's eleven-year-old daughter what we looked like at her age. When I turned the class photo over I found again the place where my teacher had signed it almost thirty years before.

Dear Betty Benz, You've been great *to know—have fun! Susie McHugh.*

KATHY BRICCETTI

Never worry too much about the things you can replace,
worry only about the things you can't replace.
GERALDINE EMMETT

DIGGING MY WAY OUT

N o teen is invincible. I just didn't know that. I was rebellious. And I didn't realize that the kids I was hanging out with could turn on me at any time. It was almost as if I were in a six-foot hole and my so-called "friends" threw me a spoon to slowly dig my hole deeper. I deceived my parents, let my grades slip, and lied to my best friend and everyone else who cared about me.

Even though my parents were divorced, it didn't change the fact that I still had a mother and a father who were both worried. During my usual stay at my dad's, I realized one afternoon that we were driving through an unfamiliar neighborhood. We pulled into a funeral home and I asked, "Who died?"

My dad never moved, never got out of the car. He just said, "There's someone waiting for you inside."

I walked through the doors of the funeral home. There stood a man who told me there was something he must show me. I followed him to what he called the Preparation Room. Bodies in this room were made up to look their best before the actual funeral services.

I glanced over at a body on a table. I couldn't see the face, but I noticed a toe tag. The man was explaining what went on in this room, but I wasn't listening. I had seen the first name on the tag. It was Jennifer. Since that was also my first name, I wanted to know more. Turning to my guide, I asked, "How did this girl die?"

"Drunk driving," he responded with a solemn expression on his face.

My inquisitive mind had to know the girl's last name. Curiosity got the best of me. I walked over, looked more closely at the tag, and froze as I saw the last name. It was mine.

How can this be? I'm standing here. I'm not dead.

Then the man opened a letter, handing it to me to read. It soon became apparent that this body under the sheet could have been mine. The toe tag was to simulate how it would be if I died.

Dear Daughter,

Your dad and I aren't husband and wife anymore, but we are still your mom and dad. Only we can truly understand the other's grief in losing you. If only you had chosen your friends more wisely. If only you had walked away from that car when you saw that the kids were drinking . . .

As I see you lying there so lifeless, I wish I could take your place. Why can't I be the one they will soon be laying in the ground? Your father and I will miss your vibrant laugh and wonderful sense of humor. I will miss seeing how your eyes sparkle when you are excited about something and want to share it with me. Your dad will miss that familiar page that says, "Call me quick! I've got news."

So many dreams and goals that you had. Now these will never be fulfilled because of one empty decision—one poor choice—one moment when you forgot to think before you acted. What might God have made of your life? I wonder what His plans were for you? Now we'll never know. We'll never get to see you grow into adulthood, meet your future husband, or hold out our arms to hold your first baby. It all came to a dead stop the night the car crashed into that cement embankment. I'll never be able to drive by that place again; a testimony

*to teenage rebellion—teenagers who thought they had all the answers
and risked their lives to prove it.*

*How will I ever walk by your room again and see the pretty bed-
spread and curtains that your dad bought for you? Or will I have to
take them down to be packed in a box that I can never open because I
simply cannot bear to see the things that remind me of you? How will
I explain to your sister how I let it happen? Was there something else I
should have done? Something else I should have said? Why wouldn't
you listen?*

*I know that teenagers think they have all the answers. You didn't
want to believe that your dad and I were actually young once and
faced many of the same temptations. You didn't want to believe that
what we were telling you was the truth—that smoking, alcohol, and
drugs would rob you of your life. You didn't want to believe that you
couldn't play around with those things—that even dabbling with
them was serious. You didn't want to believe that—yes—your friends
could be wrong. And now you are lying there so still. No more laughter.
No more sparkle in your eyes. Just an empty shell where our beautiful
baby girl used to live.*

If only you had walked away.

Mom

By the time the letter came to a close, I didn't know whether I
wanted to vomit or faint. My head was spinning with confusion.
I knew my parents had orchestrated this, but why? Slowly it
dawned on me. The choices I was making were affecting more
people than just me. Obviously, my parents were really upset and
concerned. And I *was* playing with my future. As I stood there
thinking about life and death, I realized that my decisions could
impact my unborn children who didn't even get a vote. I left the
funeral home determined to dig myself out of the hole.

Getting clean wasn't easy. I had horrible headaches, my
"friends" just quit calling, and I can't forget the radical mood
swings. Life wasn't pretty that summer, but we did what we had

to. My mom got me into counseling and I sought out a youth pastor to help me set some spiritual goals. My mom also made me accountable as far as my schedule. I "reported in" a lot. My dad called often to check up on me and to encourage me as I tried to turn my life around. And with their help, I made it through.

Whenever I drive past a cemetery I can't help but think of that fateful day—a day that I was given a chance to wake up. Then automatically my thoughts turn to the ones who loved me enough to show me a better way, and I look forward in anticipation to see what God has in store for my life.

JENNIFER TOMPKINS

PLUM TREES AND BUBBLE GUM

Outside the lit class, a line of
plum trees seem to be speakin'.
But after class, the clatter and chatter of
chaos in the high school halls;
shiny, just-waxed floors
so quickly trampled
by our teenage feet—
forever going, going,
shuffling, sitting, fleeing—
like a flock of pigeons
startled into instant flight,
not knowing their direction

So sometimes
any direction will do,
I think. Any answers,
however incomplete.
Just some action to soften
all the confusion and the questions
that roil too loudly—
oh way too loudly—
within the chaos that
I'm feeling

But my feet
have their own ideas.
Outside the lit class,
outside the walls and halls
that held me,
plum trees brush the skies
with blooms the color
of bubble gum.

They know something
of being young, I think,
as I still myself
to look at the sweep of trunks
and reaching branches—
all together elegant
and eternal, like an ancient
Chinese painting.

And pretty soon
I'm breathing.
And pretty soon
a knowing seeps into the corners
that once were scared.
For in one moment's breath,
as I look upon the plum tree,
I know I'm seeing Me—
both Young and Eternal,
both limbs and blossoms,
all at the same time.

No chaos, no shuffling,
no fleeing, no churning.
Just me.
Plum tree,
blooming in the stillness,
finding the place
where I brush the skies.

SHEILA STEPHENS

QUESTIONS OF THE HEART

*I*traveled through time last week.

Okay, all I really did was clean out a closet. But what I found in it took me back nearly three decades, to a day I never could quite explain.

The envelope was worn and the letter dog-eared and crumpled. It was written in pencil by a passionate young soldier who looked like Richard Gere.

It was written to me.

Mark was on an airplane when he wrote it, leaving Oregon for his army post on the eastern seaboard. In simple, transparent words, he put his heart on paper and mailed it off to me.

I remember how hard it was to get my mind around the idea that he was leaving again, flying away to the edge of another ocean. I had wondered if he would stand before that distant crashing surf and relive the turmoil of our last days together. It had not been smooth sailing, but that's who we were—wonderful, terrible, volatile—an explosion. It was heady stuff, being eighteen, being head over heels in love with someone who was anything but safe.

He planned to talk with my dad and come to an "understanding." Mark was an optimist. It would've taken a diplomat to resolve their differences. Mark and my father were both soldiers. Neither was a diplomat.

Passion was the star that Mark steered by. He was young and

unconquerable, full of dreams. Dad, on the other hand, had plenty of hard times in his rearview mirror. He was a little too worn down by the world that Mark was ready to take head on. Dad wasn't looking for his only daughter to be caught up in a whirlwind; he wanted her to be happy. They didn't know it, but they were opposite sides of the same coin.

I shook out of my reverie for a moment and reread the letter, closed my eyes, and began to journey back.

I read his words in a whisper, and then quietly, it was that day once more. Several weeks had passed since I'd received the letter from Mark. I had just graduated and was at work at a small CPA firm in St. Helens, Oregon. On my lunch break, I backed my '67 Firebird out of the long alley. As I continued to back past the parking lot for a local pub, my breath caught in my throat.

There he was, Mark, astride his beloved motorcycle. But it couldn't be, he'd left on a plane. I felt like I was having a hallucination.

So I didn't stop, because I knew I had to be seeing things. Mark's motorcycle wasn't here, it was in South Carolina. Still, I couldn't keep myself from looking back, and when I did, my eyes were filled with him.

Logic shouted no, it could only be an incredible imitation—right down to the resolute jaw, the smoldering look in his eyes, the exact color of his hair—and, of course, the motorcycle. It couldn't be him. Mark would've smiled that great crooked smile of his by now, so smug about surprising me.

My foot found the brake pedal, and my stare was locked. He looked so intently into my eyes and looked so strangely sad.

I shifted my car from reverse to drive, drawn to him. I pulled over, put the car in park, and my hand found the familiar door handle when I looked up again. I'll never know if it was logic, or apprehension, or simple doubt that persuaded me he looked less familiar. I mean, I had the letter he'd written on the plane. Mark was in South Carolina. So I backed away and drove to lunch.

But I watched out the window all through lunch, half expecting a motorcycle to career into the drive with a furious Mark aboard. I expected a tongue-lashing for not even stopping to talk. I wanted it more than anything, because I wanted him to be real.

Even as I expected all that, my practical mind dutifully reminded me that it could not have been my young wild-hearted love. I resolved to call him that night.

When I drove back to work, the young man and his motorcycle were gone.

After work, I hurried home, thinking there might be a message from him. The message that awaited me was not what I expected.

My father met me in the driveway with three words, as tears formed in his eyes.

"Mark is dead."

His words were gently spoken, not unkind. They were simply all he could manage. His heart was broken—for me.

I felt my legs go weak and my head began to spin.

"He was killed in a traffic accident," my father whispered. It happened that day, he said, in South Carolina.

My tears fell like rain on the hard concrete of the driveway.

Because I had lost him.

Because I had seen him.

Because I had passed him by.

Decades have passed, and I've relived these moments beyond measuring or counting. And I've come to realize the gift I was given—the gift of goodbye. The powerful, pensive image of the man I loved desperately, somehow reaching across more than a continent so we could look into each other's eyes one final time.

Although Mark and my father never did come to their understanding, I now visit them in the same place. They are at rest at Willamette National Cemetery in Portland, a very honorable place for two soldiers to be.

I remind myself that as long as someone is remembered with

love, they are never truly gone. And even rugged soldiers need flowers sometimes. So I bring them.

And always, I remember.

With love.

CHRISTY CABALLERO

BASEBALL'S BOND

As we left the underground subway station, huge electric signs glared. Throngs of people merged as in one motion. Dancing before me were more sounds, smells, lights, and people than I'd ever seen. My twelve-year-old frame trembled with excitement. Daddy looked at my wide eyes with a grin, "Don't ever forget this sight." My first glimpse of New York City would forever be etched in my memory.

My dad loved baseball and I was his baseball buddy. We watched the kings of the diamond on television, the New York Yankees. My dad's dream was to see them play, not just on TV, but in the flesh. If he couldn't be out there with the "Bronx Bombers," the next best thing was to be in attendance at Yankee Stadium. Daddy was a switch-hitter for a city league in our hometown. He could slide just like his pin-striped heroes. Clouds of dust, gravel, and the scrape of cleats joined him at home plate. Even if the ump bawled, *"Yer out,"* it was a glorious sight to behold.

Daddy was a salesman with quips and quotes for everyone he met. Each year his employer sponsored a contest that resulted in a trip to the city of the winner's choice. Three more times my dad won; four times he chose the "Yanks" hometown. He checked their schedule carefully to coordinate his trip with tickets to see his favorite team at home. Daddy's trip announcements always incited a riot of excitement in our family.

Leaving my mom and sister to explore Fifth Avenue, Daddy and I scrambled to my first subway ride to Yankee stadium. What an adventure for a little girl from North Carolina! As tunnels and rails sped by, I imagined what it would be like to live in this magical baseball kingdom. I could experience major league baseball, shell peanuts, and drink sodas with my dad every day.

We watched as our favorite October Boys, Mantle, Maris, Berra, and Ford, shellacked the Boston Red Sox. Daddy's expressions were comical to the fans sitting around us. He yelled, "Throw the good wood to it!" when a Yankee slugger came to bat. If the slugger struck out, his complaint rang loudly, "He had a hole in his bat!"

As we left the stadium my eyes caught sight of blond hair and a Yankee uniform rippled with muscle. There before my very eyes, signing autographs, was the "Mighty Mick."

Nudging me, Daddy urged, "Go get him to sign your program."

Red-faced, I balked.

"I'm not going to do it for you; you'll regret this," Daddy replied with disappointment.

The memory of those regrets has cured me of a timid demeanor. The courage to step up to life's home plate emerged from that moment. I learned to be bold enough to make an attempt at challenges beyond my comfort zone.

Later in life, my dad infected my son, Mike, with the love of the game. Mike and I collected baseball cards together. We drove to Atlanta to see another team play at their home stadium. We shelled peanuts, cheered our favorite sluggers, and booed the bad calls. I'm reminded of another bond forged years ago in another ballpark. The leathery smell of a baseball glove forever sparks those memories. Daddy's no longer with us, but each time I attend a baseball game, I feel the grand slam homer of love that a twelve-year-old girl's heart still holds for her daddy.

ANN L. COOGLER

MORE CHOCOLATE STORIES?

Do you have a true short story you want published that fits the essence of *Chocolate for a Teen's Dreams* or *Chocolate for a Teen's Heart?* I am planning future editions using a similar format which will feature stories of love, overcoming obstacles, following our intuition, divine or embarrassing moments, and humorous stories that teach us to laugh at ourselves. I am seeking touching stories of two to four pages in length that warm our hearts and encourage us to learn and grow.

I invite you to join me in these future projects by sending your special true story for consideration. If your story is selected, you will be paid $100.00, you'll be listed as a contributing author, and a biographical paragraph about you will be included. For more information or to send a story, please contact:

Kay Allenbaugh
P. O. Box 2165
Lake Oswego, Oregon 97035

Or visit my website, www.chocolateforwomen.com, and read the sample stories under "Teen Stories," then e-mail me your true story.

kay@allenbaugh.com

CONTRIBUTORS

BURKY ACHILLES is an Oregon-based writer, editor, and mother of two teenagers. She's the recipient of a Walden Fellowship and Soapstone Residency for Women Writers. She recently earned her master's in writing at Portland State University and is working on her first novel about growing up in Hawaii.

DANIELLE ARMITAGE lives in Indianapolis with her father. She is a student at Indiana University–Purdue University Indianapolis where she is studying computer science and business management. She also hopes to work toward a master's in writing. She works for Claire's Accessories and spends her free time with her family.

LINDA ASPENSON-BERGSTROM lives in Wisconsin with her two children, Hannah and Beau, and her husband, Jeff, who inspire and support her crazy lifestyle. She is a freelance artist and author currently working on a personal book of short stories, some of which she wrote as features stories while a newspaper editor. She also has a series of children's books in the works. She sells her artwork at a gallery in Wisconsin and teaches art through a community education program. She soon will be marketing a series of Christmas ornaments she designed, inspired by her kids. She remains free of anorexia through the love and support of her family and a series of self-developed life

management skills. She welcomes *anyone* in need of support to
e-mail: lindapaints@hotmail.com

BETTY AUCHARD is a retired art teacher and now writes and
speaks about tales of her childhood during the Depression, as well
as humorous and poignant stories of adjusting to widowhood.
Her entertaining and inspirational presentations are well received
by her audiences. btauchard@aol.com

DIANE GONZALES BERTRAND models the creative writing process to her students by writing and publishing her own essays,
novels, and poetry. She is the author of *Lessons of the Game, Trino's
Choice,* and *Sweet Fifteen,* all published by Arte Publico Press
in Houston, Texas. She dedicated her new novel, *Trino's Time,* to
the history professor who inspired her story in this book. She
teaches writing at St. Mary's University in San Antonio, Texas.
Dbertrand@stmarytx.edu

MAUREEN A. BOTHE is a freelance writer currently penning two
novels: a Victorian romance and a contemporary inspirational romance. Her website, www.maureenbothe.com, was a top ten fi-
nalist in Writer's Digest's Best Writer's Site Competition 2001. She
sends thanks to her sister Christine for helping her survive her
camp experience. jadrien@satx.rr.com

KATHY BRICCETTI has published her personal essays, opinion
pieces, and feature stories in newspapers, magazines, and on public radio. Her memoir, *Blood Strangers,* chronicles the saga of four
generations touched by adoption as well as her multiple journeys
to find lost family members and reestablish broken ties. She lives
with her partner and their two sons in the San Francisco Bay Area.
kbriccetti@attbi.com

RENIE SZILAK BURGHARDT, who was born in Hungary and came to the United States in 1951, is a freelance writer. Some publications in which her work has appeared are *Angels On Earth*, *Mature Living*, *Fate*, *Cat Fancy*, *Midwest Living*, *Nostalgia*, *The Friend*, and others. She resides in Doniphan, Missouri. Renie@clnet.net

APRIL BURK enjoys spending time at home in Archer, Florida, with her husband, Samuel P. Clark, and their daughters, Kayla and Sophie. She loves reading, walking, bicycling, movies, and writing. Her stories have appeared in the anthologies *A 5th Portion of Chicken Soup for the Soul*, *Forks in the Road*, *Mother Voices*, and *Pandemonium, or Life With Kids* (re-released as *I Killed June Cleaver*). Her magazine writing includes *ByLine*, *Florida Living*, *Hip Mama*, *Mothering*, *Parents*, and *Welcome Home*.

CHRISTY CABALLERO is a freelance writer and photographer who lives in a quiet forested area in the Pacific Northwest. She writes for magazines, newspapers, rescue groups, and herself, and is most in her element on a woodland trail, beside the river, or at the ocean. She writes about matters of the heart and her love for animals—large, small, pets, and wildlife. Her special bond with animals began with the massive German shepherd who decided she belonged to him the day after she was born in Anchorage, Alaska. She says The Great American Novel is, of course, in the works. greeneyz@cport.com

MICHELE WALLACE CAMPANELLI enjoys the part she's playing in creating a national bestselling Chocolate series. Author of many short stories and novels, she finds writing an outlet for artistic expression. Her novel, *Keeper of the Shroud*, was published in spring 2002 by Hollis Americana books. To contact her for more stories or comments, please go to www.michelecampanelli.com

TALIA CARNER is a novelist. Her novel *Puppet Child* was published in summer 2002. Her short stories have appeared in *Rosebud, Midstream, Moxie,* and other literary reviews. Her personal essays have appeared in *The New York Times, Lilith, Glory* (9/11), and *Happy Times Monthly* among many others. Please check her website, www.TaliaCarner.com or contact her at TaliaCarner@aol.com.

ANN L. COOGLER enjoys life in Salem, South Carolina, with her husband, Bill. She is a mother, grandmother, and former teacher. She contributes humorous writing to Writer's Ink writing group and a variety of publications. Her story is written to God's glory. (864) 944–1314; abcoog@mindspring.com

JENNIFER DOLOSKI lives in north central Illinois with her husband, Michael, daughters, Rebecca and Anna, a cat, and a dog. An at-home mom and freelance writer, she writes feature articles, essays, and short stories. doloski@yahoo.com

BETH DUNCAN is an avid writer and has set a goal to empower as many women as possible through personal contact, her short stories, and a book of poetry on which she is currently working. She lives in North Carolina with her three children, two of whom are in college. gingerfreeze11@hotmail.com

CANDIS FANCHER finds joy, fun, and gratitude in being surrounded by family and friends who give her permission to be a forever-teen at heart. She is a speech-language pathologist in the Fairview-University Health Care System in Minnesota. cfchocchips@hotmail.com

RACHAEL FEDERICO is a fifteen-year-old ninth grader at Fremont Jr. High in Mesa, Arizona. She enjoys learning, reading, writing, and listening to music. She is an active participant on the school track team. Friends and family play a big role in her life as well as giving her inspiration and self-esteem in whatever she does. A lot of her time is spent studying and working toward achieving new goals. In seventh grade, she started The Service Club at her school to aid needy children in Nepal, and she has been the club president since. She is college-bound with high hopes for the future as a writer and student. Prncessrach@aol.com

LYSSA FRIEDMAN is a freelance writer living in Mill Valley, California. As a teenager, she learned that cars, books, music played loud, and the sound of the ocean contribute meaning to life. It wasn't until she grew up, though, that she learned the value of showing up on time and studying algebra.

DAWN GOLDSMITH is a multi-published writer of non-fiction, short stories, and essays, and she also reviews books for *Publishers Weekly* and Crescent Blues eMagazine. www.crescentblues.com

MELISSA GREENE lives in Iowa on her beautiful acreage of farmland. Her hobbies include being outside, writing, music, and horseback riding. She raises show rabbits, horses, and cattle. m3lissa_lynn@hotmail.com

BETSY O'BRIEN HARRISON is a freelance writer from the northern suburbs of beautiful Pittsburgh, Pennsylvania. She has been writing for several years, but only recently in a professional arena. She has written for several e-zines and websites, as well as magazines such as *Whispers From Heaven*. Her greatest sources of inspiration are her husband, children, and parents. bobrienharrison@hotmail.com

LANA ROBERTSON HAYES, who has a master's in education, has authored many humorous essays and articles, as well as the Sonoran Sampler column in *Arizona Garden Magazine*. In a world divided by those who see the glass half empty or half full, she alone is left wondering why she received the glass with the lipstick on the rim, and who left it there. Britishtea@aol.com

CINDY KAUFFMAN is a weekly humorist in Green, Ohio, where she lives with her husband and four children. She has written more than 200 printed columns and was previously published in *Chocolate for a Woman's Dreams.* CinKau75@aol.com

SHIRLEY KAWA-JUMP and her husband, Jeff, live in Indiana with their children, Mandy and Derek. She spends her days writing and running after the kids, trying to contain messes and maintain her sanity. A fan of happy endings, she is the author of two non-fiction books and also writes for Silhouette Romance. shirley@shirleykawa-jump.com; www.writingcorner.com

KRISTIN DREYER KRAMER started writing at age ten when she, her cousin, and their two Cabbage Patch Kids formed the Poo Authors' Club. After wading through three years in an advertising agency, she escaped, became a freelance writer, and married a great guy named Paul. She is the editor-in-chief of NightsAndWeekends.com and the author of a number of humorous articles, which she swears she's going to publish in her very own book someday. And somewhere, in the back of a closet, she still has her prom dress. krdrkr@hotmail.com

SUSAN LaMAIRE is a graduate of Bucknell University where she enjoys visiting on vacations. She is a former high school English teacher who prefers making a living as a full-time waitress and part-time bookseller. While her life thus far has not been easy, she prides herself in turning the traumatic into the dramatic by retelling the story on her terms. She has previously been published in *Chocolate for a Woman's Heart* and *Chocolate for a Lover's Heart* and is currently working on her first novel. She resides in an overly pink apartment in Brick, New Jersey, and enjoys eating

Samoa Girl Scout cookies, using her free cell phone minutes, and anything Disney. (732) 477–0407

HEATHER V. LONG is a freelance writer who resides in Virginia. When she is not working hard on writing assignments, she is working on quilts and spending time with her husband, Scott, and daughter, Cassidy. Currently working on her first novel, she also raises horses and manages four dogs, three cats, and a tank full of fish. heatherlong@aol.com; www.heatherlong.com

CATHERINE MADERA is a freelance writer and mother of two. She enjoys writing essays and short stories. In addition to the Chocolate series, her work has been published by *Victoria* magazine. She lives in northwest Washington and, besides writing, enjoys gardening, reading, and horseback riding. She still believes what she learned as a teen: "There is nothing better for the inside of a man (or woman!) than the outside of a horse." res07883@gte.net

CHRIS MIKALSON lives with her husband in Alberta, Canada, and has two daughters and three grandchildren: two girls and a boy. She works full-time as a bookkeeper for a car dealership. On weekends and evenings, when not spending time with the grandkids, she pursues her love of writing. She has had articles published in *Grandparents Today* and *Woman's World* and writes for the "Soapbox" of her local newspaper. Her biggest project, a romance novel, is waiting for its second draft. i-mik@telusplanet.net

CAROL SJOSTROM MILLER lives in New Jersey with her husband, Jack, and daughters, Stephanie and Lauren. Looking for something quiet to do during her daughter's naps, she started writing and hasn't looked back. Now a nationally published freelance writer, her articles, essays, and humor pieces have appeared in *Pregnancy, Baby Years, Women's Health & Fitness, ByLine, Skirt! Magazine,* WritersDigest.com, *The Christian Science Monitor,* and many other publications. When she can find the time, she takes classes toward her master's degree in English and publishing at Rosemont College, and she hopes to finish graduate school before her kids do. miller_carol@usa.net

CAROLE MOORE is a writer and newspaper columnist based in North Carolina. A former police officer, she has also worked in television news and as a radio talk show host. Married and the mother of two, she is the author of The Perils of Eileen serialized fiction, which is carried on her website: www.thehumorwriter.com; carolemoore@ec.rr.com

DIANE PAYNE teaches creative writing at the University of Arkansas-Monticello. Burning Tulips, her memoir about growing up in Holland, Michigan, was published by Red Hen Press in 2002.

LESLEY QUINN is a freelance business and technical writer and editor who lives in the San Francisco Bay Area. Her essays have appeared in The New York Times, Brain, Child, and Skirt! Magazine. She is now at work on her first book-length manuscript. lesley@qua.com; www.lesleyquinn.com

TAMEKIA REECE is a twenty-one-year-old freelance writer residing in Houston, Texas. She enjoys reading, writing, and traveling. With her story, "Without Him," she hopes to inspire young women to realize their self-worth and potential. She can be reached and welcomes mail at tekareece@yahoo.com.

LISA SANDERS is a stay-at-home mom to two preschoolers, Torri and Teague. She says her husband, Rich, is her best friend, boyfriend, and one true love. Although she no longer stands in front of a classroom, this former teacher believes she has "chalk dust on the sleeve of her soul." A nationally published freelance writer, she specializes in family and education articles. Samples of her work can be viewed at her website: www.Joy-Writer.com; Lisa@Joy-Writer.com

HARRIET MAY SAVITZ is an author and essayist who brings inspirational fiction and non-fiction to her readers. Her books (more than twenty-one to date) help both young adolescents and adults rediscover life with all its possibilities. Her latest book, *Messages From Somewhere* (Little Treasure Publications) was released in 2002. An earlier book, *Growing Up At 62* is also published by Little Treasure Publications. One of her books, *Run, Don't Walk* (Y/A; reissued), was an ABC Afterschool Special produced by Henry Winkler. hmaysavitz@aol.com; www.harrietmaysavitz.com

ALAINA SMITH is a writer. Although she works part-time as a legal assistant, her heart belongs to her primary passion: creative writing. Besides having contributed multiple stories to the Chocolate series, she has completed a novel and is currently seeking an agent. She lives in the Northwest with her loving and supportive husband, Frank. writersmith@yahoo.com

JOYCE STARK was born and lives on the northeast coast of Scotland. She recently attended an open learning course on how to get published. She's had short stories, non-fiction, and travel articles published in the United States and the United Kingdom. She is currently working on her first novel. She and her husband, Eric, have three cats and love to travel. She says her writing "is a bit like Chicago's O'Hare—masses of ideas on the ground, some taking off and heaps more circulating and waiting to land!" joric.stark@virgin.net

SHEILA STEPHENS is an international award-winning poet, writing teacher, columnist, and speaker who enjoys helping people build their lives "from the inside out." To her, self-esteem is a spiritual journey of accepting the seed of love that divine spirit places in each heart. She has just completed *Walking With the Flowers: 50 Weeks of Quiet Meditations for a Woman's Busy World*. Her professional services include creativity coaching, personalized correspondence writing classes (available worldwide), and "Walking With the Flowers" seminars.

KATHLEEN STURGEON still occasionally trembles at podiums, but finds writing very un-traumatic. Her nonfiction articles have appeared in the Randolph Air Force Base *Wingspread, Living & Learning*, Air Force News Online, the *Renaissance*. The Kelly Air Force Base *Observer,* the *Alamo Area Horse Gazette,* and *Chocolate for a Teen's Heart*. She's currently penning an inspirational novel set in 1880's Texas. klsturgeon@aol.com

JENNIFER TOMPKINS is a seventeen-year-old high school graduate who enjoys music, running, and hanging out with her friends. She is currently attending Southern Nazarene University.

MELISSA SANDY VELA is currently twenty-one years old and lives in San Antonio, Texas. She is a senior at St. Mary's University, working toward her BA in the field of English/communication arts. Her poetry has been published in many anthologies, journals, and her hometown newspaper. This is her second essay to be published in the Chocolate series. She is currently planning her wedding to a loving man who helped her realize true beauty could never come from just a pant size. She hopes to always feel the peace and accomplishment writing gives her and wishes to continue to create art through the simple scribbles of her pen across paper. vela101@hotmail.com

PEGGY VINCENT is a retired midwife who has welcomed more than 2,500 babies into the world. She lives in Oakland, California, with Roger, her husband of thirty-six years, and Skylar, their teenage son. Two adult children, Colin and Jill, live nearby. Her first book, *BABY CATCHER: Chronicles of a Modern Midwife,* was released in the spring of 2002 by Scribner. In addition to working on a sequel, she also writes fiction and short essays. Visit her website at www.babycatcher.net and sign the guest book, or send her an e-mail at PV@peggyvincent.com.

FERIDA WOLFF is the author of *Listening Outside Listening Inside,* an inspirational book for adults about listening to your inner messages. She is also the author of more than a dozen books for children and young adults. Her work has been published in newspapers, magazines, and literary journals. She has an MS in education and is certified in holistic studies. She taught yoga and leads meditation workshops. fwolff@erols.com; www.feridawolff.com

SHARON WREN is a freelance writer who lives on an island on the Mississippi River with her husband, Bud, sons Logan and Tyler, five dachshunds, two cats, and more geese and ducks than she can count. She enjoys writing about humor, parenting, writing, gardening, and cooking. swren1@msn.com; http://i.am/overworkedandunderpaid

LYNNE LAYTON ZIELINSKI lives in Huntsville, Alabama. A freelance writer, she believes that life is a gift from God, and what we do with it is our gift to God. She has a seventeenth-century historical novel in progress. (256) 883–1592. Arisway@aol.com

ACKNOWLEDGMENTS

My heartfelt thanks to the contributors of this book for sharing their memorable and poignant true stories, and for the joy they brought into my life. It is a gift to be able to see through their young eyes the enormous opportunities and challenges they experience.

Many, many thanks to my agent, Peter Miller, and his staff as they routinely promote the Chocolate series and sing its praises, making sure books are available around the world.

All good things to my editor, Caroline Sutton, for her expertise and the tireless efforts of the entire crew at Fireside/Simon & Schuster who are working behind the scenes stirring and growing the Chocolate mix. I appreciate you all!

On the home front, hugs and kisses to my young-at-heart husband, Eric, our sons, their wives, and our new grandbabies! Life is rich, indeed.

Enormous thanks to my administrative support, Jan Richardson and Tamara Johnson, for making Chocolate a priority in their lives.

Kudos goes to Sarah Hall Productions, Inc. and Elise Marshall in raising the visibility bar for the Chocolate series.

To my dear friends, much love. Thank you for teaching me how to play on a regular basis.

May all your lives be blessed, and may you continue to be young at heart!

ABOUT THE AUTHOR

Kay Allenbaugh is the author of *Chocolate for a Woman's Soul, Chocolate for a Woman's Heart, Chocolate for a Lover's Heart, Chocolate for a Mother's Heart, Chocolate for a Woman's Spirit, Chocolate for a Teen's Soul, Chocolate for a Woman's Blessings, Chocolate for a Teen's Heart, Chocolate for a Woman's Dreams, Chocolate for a Teen's Spirit* and *Chocolate for a Woman's Courage.* She resides with her husband, Eric Allenbaugh, Ph.D. (author of *Wake-Up Calls: You Don't Have to Sleepwalk Through Your Life, Love or Career;* and *Deliberate Success: Realize Your Vision with Purpose, Passion, and Performance*), in Lake Oswego, Oregon.

Look for the other volumes
of delicious Chocolate stories